Bringing
TALENTED
CHILD

To Julia —
May yours turn
out better then
my mothers'

Paula

Published by Bay Books
61–69 Anzac Parade
Kensington NSW 2033

© Geoffrey Lewis
Cartoons by Stephen Scheding

National Library of Australia
card number and ISBN 1 86256 322 5

BB 88

Printed in Singapore by Toppan Printing Company.
Typeset by Savage Type Pty Ltd, Brisbane, Australia.

The publisher would like to thank the following for
their assistance and advice during the production of this
book: Ms Julie Campbell, Institute of Early Childhood
Studies, Newtown, NSW; Dr Yvonne Larson, School of
Teaching and Curriculum Studies, University of
Sydney, Sydney, NSW; and Ingaret Ward, editor.

Bringing up your TALENTED CHILD

Geoffrey Lewis

Cartoons by Stephen Scheding

BAY BOOKS
Sydney and London

This book is dedicated to my elder daughter, Georgia, who introduced me to the world of the gifted and talented, and to her sister, Myfwny, who kept me there.

ABOUT THE AUTHOR

Geoff Lewis's career as a teacher has taken him to many schools throughout New South Wales, the Australian Capital Territory and Britain teaching history, English, remedial language and special courses for talented children.

He now works for the New South Wales Department of Education as a regional consultant for the education of children with special talents.

His years as a liaison officer for children, their families, schools and community organisations, have given him experience sorting out problems and finding new ways to develop a child's maximum potential in the best way possible.

CONTENTS

1
HOW DO YOU IDENTIFY A TALENTED CHILD?

A child
is
a child
is
a child..

Why a Book about Talented Children?

All children are special to someone. Some children also have special talents. This book is for parents who think their child might be gifted and who want to learn more about this area in order to foster the development of those special talents.

Talent exists in many forms and to varying degrees. The reaction of parents to talent also varies: from pride and delight, to fear and reluctance.

Parents of a talented child have certain responsibilities, not only in identifying potential and actual talent but in nurturing and extending that talent. You and your child's school can work co-operatively in encouraging your child and in meeting her/his needs. Talent can be enjoyable and enriching for your child, you and the community if you remember the golden rule: your child is a child first, a talented person second.

In Australia today, there is a growing realisation that, while worthy efforts have been made to help under-privileged and disabled children, less has been attempted at the other end of the scale. Efforts are now being made to redress this imbalance. Every child should receive an education geared to their particular gifts and talents.

A quick word on the general meanings of gifted and talented may be useful. Although in common speech these words are used interchangeably, in some education systems 'gifted' is used to describe children with exceptional abilities in many areas, while 'talented' is used to describe children with ability in a specific or perhaps two related areas. So a gifted child may have exceptional ability in several subjects, for example, language, mathematics, science and sport. A talented child may be exceptional in language or art or music, but not all of them. Throughout this book, however, we have chosen to use the terms interchangeably.

How Do You Define Talent?

During the first half of the twentieth century, researchers into education and psychology began to examine the concept of giftedness. As a result, many definitions and a huge, sometimes confusing list of criteria have emerged.

The first solid research was by an American psychologist, Lewis M Terman, who followed a group of children he had identified as 'gifted and talented' from school to middle age. He based his definition on the fact that his subjects had scored above 150 on a standard intelligence test. During this long study, from 1925 to the late 1950s, he tried to work out what made these children gifted.

His research, based on white, middle class families, appeared to show that talented children:

☆ excelled in all areas of intellectual development and performance;

☆ were highly motivated to learn and achieve;

☆ could all handle language well;

☆ were mature, independent and self-directed.

Terman's theories became the basis for research and the teaching of talented children for decades. When you were at school, the 'bright' kids were probably those who had been identified as having a 'high IQ' (although no one ever found out what this magic number actually was) and they were often held up as models for other children to follow.

By the 1970s, new questions were being asked about many of the assumptions underlying the whole talented child area. Surely, for example, children from a variety of economic and ethnic backgrounds could be just as talented as Terman's group? Where do you cut off the IQ score to distinguish between the 'talented' and the 'non-talented'? (It's a bit like trying to define 'tall' and 'not tall'!) Educationists began to question the validity of IQ tests as the sole basis for judging intelligence. The very nature of these tests seemed to discriminate against those minority groups for whom English was not a first language. Many went so far as to question seriously whether such tests really did test what they were supposed to test — certain thinking and reasoning skills, for example.

Where do you cut off the IQ score?

Quite a dilemma! If talent can't be defined alone by IQ tests or intellectual ability, how can it be defined? Here are four broad definitions.

1. Talent can be described by looking at history and people with outstanding achievements of some kind. This is called an *ex post facto* definition (after the fact).

2. Another way is to assume that a certain percentage of the population will be talented in relation to the intellectual ability of the general population. Again, the problem emerges of where to draw the line. Terman suggested that the top 2 per cent of the population is gifted. Others have thought the top 10 per cent, while others still believe that 20 per cent will include all talented people. This is called a *percentage* definition.

3. Probably the most common way is to describe talent in terms of performance in one or more tests of general intelligence — the so-called IQ tests. This is called a *psychometric* definition.

4. Another way considers a wide range of factors such as behaviour, creativity, performance, special ability or even potential in many areas of worthwhile human endeavour. This is known as a *multi-faceted* or *multi-criteria* definition.

Today more children are being identified as talented.

Today, most definitions of 'gifted and talented' use the last approach — they have broadened from the very narrow basis of intellectual performance, to a much wider basis encompassing many areas of achievement. Most importantly, this means that more children are being identified as talented.

INTELLECTUAL CHARACTERISTICS

Being self-motivated to learn, discover and explore.

Being independent in thought and action, well-organised and goal-directed.

Having a long attention span and an excellent memory.

Having keen powers of observation.

Being capable of single-minded determination.

Being self-critical with high standards for own performance.

Having a large vocabulary, fluently used.

Seeking out a challenge and responding to new ideas; correspondingly bored with routine and repetition.

Having a wide range of hobbies and interests, usually at a sustained level of interest sometimes a year or more ahead of children of the same age.

Having a preference for games giving scope for careful thought or vivid imagination.

Identifying Talented Children

Identifying talented children is a continuous and sometimes difficult process, using many criteria and starting at an early age. Talent may only reveal itself when a child encounters an experience which taps a latent interest or ability.

A great deal of research into this area has resulted in lists of intellectual and social characteristics to look for. Although far from definitive, these lists may help parents to identify a talented child with some accuracy. Of course, a talented child may have only a few of the characteristics listed.

In my teaching career and work as a consultant, I have noticed that some characteristics seem to occur more frequently than others, so I'll discuss them in a little more detail.

Identifying talented children is a continuous process.

11

Play

Quite often you may notice that a younger child prefers to play with older children, especially in challenging, complicated games and activities. A younger child may even take over a game. Sometimes this is resented by the other children, but usually they accept a younger child if they find that he or she has something worthwhile to contribute. By itself, the desire to play with older children is not necessarily an indication of unusual ability, but if that child also mixes and converses confidently with adults, he/she may be talented. It is quite likely that he or she is a gifted child.

Humour

Gifted children often have a delightful sense of humour. A child with a fine sense of irony or a rather wry, dry wit could well be talented. At a relatively early age, such children will read and appreciate the humour in the novels, poems and short stories of Roald Dahl, for example. Later, they may enjoy the work of Spike Milligan or the Monty Python team. They will be amused, especially if the humour is ironic or satirical, by something other children of their age might not find funny.

Sensitivity to Others

This may appear indirectly in the child's willingness to do things like organising charity collections at school. More obviously talented children tend to speak out against injustice to themselves or to others. Many such children are socially or politically aware at an early age. They have little difficulty in empathising with other people, feeling strongly for the plight of anyone in trouble. Bright children often stand up for their rights or for those of other people in an almost aggressive way.

Children need success and recognition and can be very sensitive to criticism. For the same reason they may also be vulnerable if rejected by their peer group. This is particularly true of talented children.

They may also spend time 'day dreaming', especially if they are artistically talented children. This behaviour can be misinterpreted as a lack of concentration, but often, these children are simply interested in the more human and aesthetic aspects of the world and need time to think.

Artistically talented children may spend time day dreaming.

SOCIAL CHARACTERISTICS

Being co-operative at home or at school.

Being friendly and outgoing, sensitive to other people and their needs.

Having a highly developed sense of humour, often ironic.

Choosing older playmates.

Conversing easily and well with adults and discussing matters in an 'adult' way.

Having a highly developed sense of social and moral responsibility, challenging decisions that may be considered unfair and supporting other people in trouble.

Having a tendency to be modest about achievements or to accept them as normal; sometimes seeking to hide ability, especially if peer pressure is applied not to conform to adult rules.

Independence in Activities and Learning

Another frequent characteristic of gifted children is being able to work independently on a project or hobby. This kind of ability, accompanied by outstanding powers of concentration and memory, is a sure sign of talent. Many teachers, parents and grandparents tell of children who, from an early age, could occupy themselves in constructive play for 'hours at a time'. Nothing would disturb their concentration. Children like this are often able to recall, in minute detail, events that happened long before. It becomes clear that these children can also remember a great deal of information in a short period of time. A word of warning here: in a number of cases, especially among talented primary children, it's necessary to teach the skills of independent study and research. They do not necessarily come automatically.

The skills of independent study can be taught.

Boredom

Talented children easily become bored with repetitive routine, the obvious or the mundane. This is, of course, one of the great challenges for teachers and parents! These children must be extended and enriched.

It is a great injustice when teachers and parents give more-of-the-same in an effort to encourage talent. Bright children do not appreciate doing twenty extra long divisions just because they are good at long division. It may well seem to them that they are being punished for being clever. It is far better to give these children a long and more complicated problem to which they can apply their skills.

Children must be extended and enriched.

In order to avoid boredom, talented children often find new ways to solve problems. Children with linguistic talent will try to write in different and appropriate styles using unusual words; while the artistically talented will be excited at the prospect of trying a different art medium, or finding a new way of expressing an old idea.

Language

Many talented children have advanced vocabularies. They use language with skill and flexibility. They are fluent, creative and confident in their written and oral language. They take pleasure in 'playing' with words and investigating their subtleties and possibilities.

Talented children use language with skill and flexibility.

Hobbies

Some talented children show great versatility and virtuosity and can adapt readily to new challenges. Many have a wide range of interests and hobbies.

Knowledge

Bright children have great intellectual curiosity. They're always asking 'Why?' They try to find the cause/effect relationships and can easily grasp the underlying principles of an issue.

Being able to think critically allows these children to get to the nub of a problem. They are sceptical, evaluative and often self-critical. They learn quickly and may have an extensive general knowledge which outstrips that of many adults. They often have extremely long attention and concentration spans, as well as an excellent memory for information and experiences. They can be very persistent in their pursuit of knowledge, overcoming any obstacles to achieve their goal.

Keen powers of observation allow talented children to note detail and see similarities and differences in a situation. This leads to seeing what is significant and being interested in the unusual rather than the conventional. They may also be stimulated by discussing what might be regarded as 'adult' problems and issues — religion, politics, injustice, race.

Although many bright children have free-wheeling, creative minds, most like some structure and order. Like all children, they need consistency. This is especially so of mathematically gifted children who are interested in value and number systems, clocks and calendars. Many invent their own systems. Paradoxically,

A talented child may need extra help.

some children can be quite inflexible in their attitudes and may need help coming to terms with other people's rules or expectations.

Physical Characteristics

Extraordinary co-ordination, agility, fitness, speed and stamina are all traits of the talented sportsperson. Experts have also identified some traits that seem to apply generally to gifted people, although I have not yet seen any conclusive evidence to support such a theory. These experts claim that gifted children should:

☆ be slightly heavier and taller than their peers;

☆ be somewhat stronger and healthier than other children the same age;

☆ be relatively free of physical and nervous disorders; mature physically at an earlier age;

☆ as infants, reach milestones such as toilet training earlier than their brothers and sisters.

These claims seem debatable. It is true that children in good general health are likely to get more out of life because good physical health stimulates good mental health. Yet I have met several talented children who are smaller, lighter and less physically mature than their siblings and friends but are streets ahead intellectually.

Co-ordination, agility, fitness, speed and stamina are all traits of being talented at sport.

TALENT IN SPORT

Enjoying and performing outstandingly in physical activities.

Physically co-ordinated and graceful in movement.

Liking many sports and encouraging others to join in.

Spending a great deal of time in practice or training.

Reading magazines and books on sport or recreational activities.

Being highly competitive.

Having the ability to 'read' a game, especially in team sports.

Talented Handicapped Children

A word or two on talented children with disabilities or handicaps is important here. My mother claimed that 'Nature always seems to compensate for a disability or handicap!' Somehow, I think this is often true.

I know of a lad who was born with a severely deformed foot, making some physical activities impossible. As 'compensation', he is a gifted artist who also enjoys being the scorer for the local cricket team. He has an encyclopaedic knowledge of cricket as an additional bonus. As another example, I know a girl with *spina bifida* who was dux of her large high school.

A handicap is not a bar to being talented. As parents, it is natural to make some compensation if a child has a disability or handicap. In many cases this is necessary for the safety and well-being of the child. These children may need more encouragement to boost their self-esteem. There are handicapped people who are extremely talented in areas not affected by their disability. These

people work hard to overcome their disability and achieve great things. Think of the blind people who perform brilliantly at university or in their chosen career, for example.

Alternatively, within the context of the handicapped there are those who win gold medals at the Handicapped Olympics. The ability and determination shown by these athletes place them in the ranks of the talented by any criteria.

Talented Children Are not Perfect

Talented children are just like other children: some are well behaved and others are not. Some may have characteristics which may be misinterpreted by adults, such as hyperactivity. Some talented children may not be recognised as such, due to social problems, such as stammering, or emotional problems, which may cause temporary withdrawal. A talented child may need extra help to overcome any difficulties. This is discussed in detail later in the book.

Talented children are just like other children: some are well-behaved and others are not.

POOR INTERPERSONAL SKILLS

Impatience or intolerance with people unable to 'keep up'.

Poor self-image especially in older children through fear that their skills may be rejected by peers as 'showing off'.

Use of humour as a weapon to criticise or mock others.

Inability to accept the opinion of others through arrogance or rigidity.

FRUSTRATION WITH OTHERS

Not feeling challenged enough.

Feeling isolated — misunderstood or not taken seriously by others, especially adults.

Feeling let down by situations that do not meet expectations of excellence.

FRUSTRATIONS WITH SELF

Disorganised attention to too many areas of interest.

Overexpenditure of energy.

Inability to meet unrealistic goals.

2
TYPES OF TALENT

Identifying areas of potential talent will help you plan your child's education at home, at school and in the community. It may also affect your expectations of your child, since the child is born with certain talents and it helps if you respond to what is given. In other words, you may find yourself nurturing an artist rather than the mathematical genius you always wanted to be yourself. It is very important to put aside your own ambitions and focus on your child's needs.

Specific or General Talent

Genuine all-round giftedness is very rare indeed. I haven't encountered more than a dozen examples in almost twenty years of teaching. Yet in my job as a consultant I regularly meet children with very specific talents. These children may be gifted in maths and science yet have trouble putting words together to make a sentence; others may read at levels way above their years and use language as effectively as any adult, but have difficulty with maths. Some talented children may even need help in areas where they do not show ability. If talents are related, it's usually in such areas as maths and science, language and history, maths and music, for example.

Genuine all-round giftedness is very rare indeed.

How the Specialists View Talent

Australian education authorities, using the broad definition of talent discussed in the last chapter, have identified several different areas:

Intellectual: the ability to think logically, abstractly or divergently (widely) at higher levels than most people.

Creative: the ability to think in unusual patterns that may be unique and original.

Academic: excellence at specific or closely related basic school subjects such as language, maths, science, history, English, art.

Specialist: involvement in additional activities and hobbies outside school, such as classification of rocks or stamps, using computers and so forth.

Social: strong leadership skills, often revealed at an early age when playing games with other children.

Physical: a high level of skill in movement, grace, co-ordination, the ability to 'read the game', the motivation and commitment needed for long hours of training.

There are many different areas of talent.

DRAMATIC TALENT

Early ability to role-play or mimic realistically.

Great satisfaction in dramatic performances — this child is often the first to volunteer for the class or school play if given the opportunity.

Understanding dramatic conflict.

Writing original scripts.

Keen observation of other people.

Interest in the technical aspects of theatre or television and in forms of drama not normally encountered by children (eg radio drama).

Performing: acting, art, music, craft, cooking, needlework and other, usually elective, subjects at high school.

Mechanical: the ability to find out how things work by taking something apart and putting it back together again correctly.

Aesthetic: the ability to think philosophically about moral, spiritual and aesthetic considerations (often accompanies talent in the visual arts or language).

ARTISTIC TALENT

From an early age, much time spent drawing, painting, using clay or plasticine.

Originality in the choice of subject, technique, composition or materials and willingness to experiment.

Use of art to express feelings — school books may be lavishly illustrated, even at the expense of written content.

Enjoyment of visits to galleries or exhibitions.

Ways of Thinking

Jargon a parent should know when dealing with the world of education.

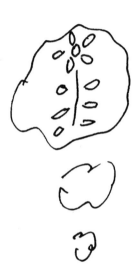

I have tried to keep this book free of jargon but in the world of education, jargon does exist. It may be useful for parents to know what this jargon means so they are not confused or intimidated by it. One phrase that crops up is 'cognitive style'. This simply means the way a person thinks, how an individual interprets an idea. Some people prefer to listen, some to watch, some to read, to solve problems or pursue new ideas. Thinking (cognitive) styles are classified in two ways: *field independent* and *field dependent*.

Field independent thinkers see something independent of the field or context surrounding it. For example, think of a flower. The field independent person would see the petals, stalk, colour, sepals and any distinctive markings. This person tends to be an analytical thinker whose interests might move towards science or mathematics.

The field dependent thinker appreciates the flower as a whole and takes into account the garden in which it grows. This global thinker's interests might include writing and other creative arts.

These styles crystallise around the age of eight. Of course, no one belongs completely to either group. Most people move between the two, depending on the circumstances, but usually one or the other style dominates. Those rare people who are multi-talented may have more of a balance between the two styles.

Why Is Cognitive Style Important?

While there is no direct relationship between type of cognitive style and degree of intelligence, your child's way of thinking may determine his/her areas of interest. It will help everyone if you realise that no one can change your child's cognitive style. It is something each one of us is born with.

It's important for parents and teachers to know how each child thinks so experiences and activities can be planned to encourage abilities and cope with problems.

Methods of working also vary. Almost by definition, talented field independent children are more self-directed and persistent, whereas field dependent children prefer to work in groups. By implication, not all talented children are suited to the kind of independent work we often expect of them.

Not all talented children are suited to independent work.

MECHANICAL TALENT

Interest in how mechanical gadgets work.

Having a hobby like radios, building kits, etc.

Handling tools competently and with good co-ordination.

Understanding puzzles and trick questions, drawing mechanical objects or plans, reading books and magazines on mechanical or scientific subjects.

Designing and building quite sophisticated, practical objects.

Above average mathematical ability, especially for practical mathematics and geometry.

In the past, creativity and giftedness were not seen as different.

What Is Creativity?

All creative people are talented, not all talented people are creative. Creativity is one of the most difficult and least understood areas. In the past, creativity and giftedness were not seen as different. People expected all talented children to be creative, and at the same time, dismissed as unintelligent those whose talents were solely in the field of the arts.

In this century, Alfred Binet, famous for his IQ test, noted that some children responded to some of the questions in his test in an unusual or unexpected way, but did not score well overall. These children were classified as being of lesser intelligence. Although Binet's discovery was made around the time of World War I, it was not until the 1950s that creativity as a separate entity was given any serious consideration by researchers. James P Guildford was a leader in this area of research, but he had one problem which has not been solved — creativity is difficult or maybe impossible to define. Here are a few attempted definitions:

'The capacity of persons to produce compositions, products or ideas of any sort which are essentially new and novel and previously unknown to the producer.'

John Devdahl, 1956

'A combination of flexibility, originality and sensitivity to new ideas which enables the thinker to move away from usual sequences of thought with different and productive sequences, the results of which he gives to himself and to others.'

J P Jones, 1972

'Giftedness is the total integrated functioning of the human brain, so creativity (is) the highest expression of giftedness.'

Barbara Clark, 1983

James Guildford noted certain traits that creative people seem to have:

- ☆ sensitivity;
- ☆ innovative ability;
- ☆ a good memory;
- ☆ a high degree of observation;
- ☆ a strong aesthetic sense;
- ☆ no concern for meticulousness or for discipline;
- ☆ self-confidence;
- ☆ impulsiveness and cheerfulness;
- ☆ an ability to relax easily;
- ☆ a keen sense of humour that is creative and original.

In the 1960s and 1970s various tests were devised to try and measure creativity. The best known were developed by Torrance, Wallach and Kogan, and Getzels and Jackson. These and others have all fallen into disrepute. No agreement was ever reached about methods of measuring, or what 'original', 'novel', 'unusual', or 'worthwhile' thinking might be. In addition, could children be expected to think creatively and spontaneously in the stress of tests? The test did not cover the process side of creativity in, say, creative problem solving: formulation of the problem, incubation, insight and evaluation. It was necessary to go back to the drawing board!

MUSICAL TALENT

Musical family background.

Natural awareness and sensibility to pitch, rhythm and volume; can associate other things with music, eg rain on the roof.

Enthusiasm in wanting to learn musical instrument and an ability to concentrate for long periods.

Reading about music and enjoying going to concerts and other musical performances.

No agreement was ever reached about methods of measuring creativity.

Identifying Creatively Gifted Children

These days, Australian educators use checklists of characteristics to help them identify creatively gifted children. The checklists in this chapter are a shortened form. They are not exhaustive and are designed to provide parents with a guide only. Most parents can learn, by watching their child, if he/she enjoys a particular activity very much and is beginning to excel at it, in comparison with the peer group or siblings.

I mention the importance of family background in the music checklist only, but of course it can be important in any area. A child who comes from a home where reading, writing and conversation are the norm, is likely to be more talented linguistically than the child who is given unlimited television watching as the main stimulus. Think of how many sports people come from 'sporting families' or how areas such as medicine and law can become family professions.

3
THE FAMILY

In the life of any child, the family plays a crucial part. This chapter looks at some specific areas of family influence.

Expectations

Parents provide the main educational model.

What a family expects from a child is a major factor in how that child makes use of his or her abilities. Home expectations may be the most important factor in a child's achievement in and out of school.

I cannot stress strongly enough how important you are as a role model for your child. Your interest in education, and in recreational and cultural pursuits is likely to be the main model your child will follow. Irrespective of the efforts made by the school, talented children will tend not to fulfil their potential if their home does not respect and encourage intellectual or creative endeavour. Families need to value perseverance, freedom of action and developing independence.

Teachers need to be aware that there may be conflict between the school and the family. Some nationalities regard independence as a threat to traditional values. Very careful and courteous communication may be needed between a school and a family to try to overcome real cultural differences which may tear the child apart.

A child first... A talented child second...

Two Golden Rules

As a parent you have a great deal of power over the development of your talented child. There are two golden rules for parents to remember:

☆ *Your talented child is a child first and a talented child second.* A talented child has the same needs as other children and should be accepted as a child.

☆ *Don't push.* Like any other child, a talented child will resent pressure. Let their talent be an enjoyable, enriching experience. Encourage your child in what he or she wants to achieve while giving them time to relax and to play. It is a vital part of growing up.

Social Life

Try to provide opportunities for your child to establish warm and accepting relationships within a wide circle of friends and acquaintances. Some children are naturally outgoing and friendly; others are shy, withdrawn and require parental patience. As they grow older, encourage children to go on excursions, camps, sporting trips or social events to learn independence.

All children have to learn to mix with a variety of people, irrespective of abilities and interests. Many talented children will become leaders later in life, and they will use their talent more effectively if they understand and accept that everyone is different. Charity and community work for older children can be a good learning experience in this area.

Again, there may be cultural clashes between home and school in the area of social expectations. For example, some religions or nationalities may not want their children taking part in camps. It is worth trying to sort out these problems, as the child eventually has to survive in the wider community.

All children have to learn to mix with a variety of people.

Stimulation

Challenge your child to think. It helps create intellectual independence. Provide situations that offer problems to solve; interesting ideas, new experiences in the arts, visits to museums and exhibitions. As far as possible, answer your child's questions directly and honestly. If you don't know the answer, say so and suggest where it may be found. Encourage your child to reach out for more information and greater self-expression. Awareness of the world grows through enriching contact.

Talented children need help in exploring and developing their interests. It's also important for them to become competent in basic skills and areas in which they may not be interested. Try to strike a balance in your child's life — offer help in those areas where the child may need extra attention. It's embarrassing for a mathematical genius to have trouble tying her shoelaces.

Answer your child's questions directly and honestly.

Reading Material

The benefits of having available a variety of books, magazines and newspapers cannot be over-emphasised. Children need this wide reading, even if it is in an area in which they already show a talent. Encourage use of the local library and try to share your child's enthusiasm for reading, without being too obtrusive or interfering.

Magazines which specialise in an interest keep the child in touch with the latest developments and issues. They help the process of obtaining deeper knowledge as well as opening up possible new avenues of research. Exposure to high quality magazines and newspapers allows the development of a critical taste in reading that is essential for gifted children. Quite often, specialised magazines can enhance a visit to a zoo, art gallery, concert or play.

Don't worry if an avid reader suddenly starts reading simpler books — the child is probably just taking a rest, relearning something or wanting to take part in their peer group.

Don't worry if an avid reader suddenly starts reading simpler books.

Independence and Responsibility

Most talented children like to try to solve their own problems and be independent. It's important for children to have space of their own where they can read, write, create and follow their interests. Respect their privacy and in return your child will learn to show the same respect for others. Perhaps more than other children, talented children often need to be alone, to contemplate, to dream and to make plans.

Children need space of their own where they can read, write, create and follow their interests.

Allow them to develop a sense of responsibility by such things as looking after pets or managing pocket money and their own possessions. Even their appearance is a possible area for skilful parental tolerance. From an early age, they are likely to choose the clothes they want from the wardrobe. Sometimes this may mean some unusual combinations! My own daughter, for instance, wore clothes pegs in her hair to school for a week or so. Don't worry about such behaviour. It will give you many pleasant memories to look back upon. Never make fun of idiosyncrasies — there is nothing wrong with wanting to be different, and your child's self-esteem is more important than conventional preconceptions.

Decision-making should be nurtured as early as possible.

Decision-making is important and should be actively nurtured as early as possible. Family situations offer countless opportunities for this. Any child who feels confident as a decision-maker is likely to have a positive self-image which will form a vitally useful foundation for the future.

Play

Like all children, talented children like to play. It is part of growing up and can be a very useful escape valve from intellectual pressure. Sometimes talented children want to over-organise other children when playing — it is a sure way to lose friends. Gently point out the importance of everyone being involved in the decision-making of play.

Enjoy the experience of playing games with your child — whether it's snakes and ladders, table tennis or chess, it can be a rewarding form of relaxation for the whole family.

Relaxation

Talented children need time to wind down and turn off, just as you may read the comics in the daily paper or watch light entertainment on television. These forms of relaxation are vital. Physical activity, too; it not only relaxes and stimulates the body, it also sharpens the mind. Help your child to strike a healthy balance in life.

Rules and Conventions

Talented children often question convention, their minds taking paths that are not so obvious to others. These are times to explain society's conventions and the importance of rules and regulations. Give practical examples, such as the need for all vehicles to travel on the same side of the road, going in the same direction. Point out that society demands courtesy and regard for the rights of others. If your child touches on areas that you or society may consider taboo, try to answer truthfully, in a forthright way. All children need genuine answers to real questions, and the talented child by his/her nature is often even more curious.

All children need genuine answers to real questions.

If you have ks and ss why do you need cs?

Tolerance

Most bright children are well aware that they can achieve more than others and usually accept this as natural and take their ability in their stride. Occasionally, a child may feel different and might even feel inferior in some way; other children can be cruel to someone they perceive as unusual. It is important for children to understand their own strengths and weaknesses and to focus on the things they do well. Help your children in a matter-of-fact way, with a young child especially, without using words like 'gifted' and 'intelligence'. Point out that all people can do some things better than others, just as some people are tall and others are short. The important thing is how people use their ability.

Tight haloes cause bad headaches.

There are so many ways in which a parent can assist a child. Keep trying — experiment with new areas without becoming a pushy parent. Don't expect a talented child to be gifted all the time in all things. Tight haloes cause bad headaches.

4
TALENTED PRE-SCHOOLERS

The Earlier the Better

Often, talent will reveal itself early in a child's life. Think back to the first chapter on the characteristics of talent and you will remember some of the indications that make these children stand out from their friends or brothers and sisters: intense concentration, persistence and an eagerness to learn, for example. It is almost axiomatic that the earlier a talent is recognised, the more likely a child will successfully develop it.

It is also axiomatic that these pre-schoolers are still children and will want to play, to climb, to explore and discover the world for themselves. They are just like other children, except that talented children do these things differently.

The earlier a gift is recognised, the more likely a child will succeed.

The years before your child starts school should provide a solid foundation for life. Don't take too much notice of books which claim that at a certain age your child should be able to do certain things. This ignores the fact that all children are different and unique. Talented children often proceed at a pace which defies all stages of behaviour expected of 'normal' children. Sometimes they may even lag behind other children. Don't worry: everyone develops in their own way.

No single method can be described as the best way to raise a gifted pre-schooler. Parents should try to enjoy their child's development and do their best to reinforce the child's efforts. Show enthusiasm to build up the child's positive self-image. Childhood is precious.

The Role of the Parent

It is certain that the child's family, as a model of behaviour, has a great influence on the pre-schooler's development. For example, children who are often read to by their parents, who are encouraged to talk and answer questions, and whose parents play with them or take them on walks or picnics, are all more likely to develop intellectually than those who are deposited in front of the television with no other stimulation. Strike a sensible balance — parental haloes can get tight too!

Parents who display a real interest in ideas or books can act as positive models for their children. Frequent and natural interaction between parent and child is a recipe for success. This also implies that parents who rely on their own resources, rather than on artificial devices, are the key to opening doors for the gifted pre-schooler.

A general characteristic of the talented is their need for independence. Beware that this is not always so, as some children have to be taught this quite explicitly. Parents who encourage independent behaviour from an early age will help their child to gain the confidence to master many of the tasks and challenges that he/she will face in life and to weather occasional setbacks.

Give responsibility at an early age. Begin by giving responsibility at an early age. Self-care and daily jobs such as making the bed or feeding the cat, will encourage independence and problem solving.

Pre-schools

For the talented, pre-school can be especially valuable. I have been a fan of pre-schools for a long time; both my children attended the local pre-school two days a week. For the talented, pre-school can be especially valuable, providing familiarity with the pleasures and 'rules' of social interaction that may not be available at home.

Another advantage is that pre-schools give children experiences that can be talked about later. In trying to share them with the rest of the family, their efforts to describe what went on at pre-school that morning call upon and extend their language resources. Listen to what your child is trying to explain or describe, and pose questions that will make him/her think a little more.

The choice of pre-school is yours. There are many options available, from a few hours a week, to full day care. Choose what you see as best for your child and family, but don't let pre-school

become a substitute for home. Watch how comfortable your child feels. Note if he/she is excited about pre-school and looks forward to going. These are good indications, as is talk about friends and activities.

Talk to the staff about what your child does at home. Anything that interests, fascinates, puzzles or disturbs is useful information for the staff. A two-way exchange of information can develop if they tell you of similar things at pre-school. They are seeing your child in a different context than the home. Such firm foundations, when started early, can be continued once your child enters school.

Don't let pre-school become a substitute for home.

Common Questions Parents Ask about Pre-schoolers

Wouldn't my child learn more at home with me?
Yes, probably. But the best parent in the world cannot provide the magical stimulus given by the company of other children in a social environment. This is not only a useful preparation for the group context of all formal education, it is a lot of fun. Adults provide wonderful entrees to the worlds of literature, art and music, but the day is probably made by being offered a turn on the swing by 'my friend'. Social understandings require intelligence, sensitivity and imagination, and can be learned playing in the park or backyard with friends. It is too easy to dismiss these activities as non-intellectual.

Is my child getting enough stimulation?

Seeing the same old equipment set out day after day may look boring for a child whom you know needs lots of stimulation. Don't underestimate the needs of all children to have the security of old favourites. They also have the ability to extend the potential of non-structured materials like water, sand, paint and pieces of wood. However, if the program at pre-school is dreary, suggest something you could contribute, like some materials for collage, or an afternoon making hats and masks if you can give the time.

Academic skills like reading, writing and numbers are sometimes acquired by children quite early. Will this worry the pre-school teacher?

Probably, although more enlightened teachers will accept it. There are still a few 'fossils' in pre-schools and kindergartens who can't cope with precocious readers. Children writing or dictating their own stories to go with paintings and drawings is a very natural way of recording experience.

Young children can be fascinated by numbers. Think how important it is for little children to know their age and how proudly they hold up one or two fingers to indicate that they know how old they are. A fascination with numbers is not necessarily an indication of talent. Watch for the young child who readily shows that he/she can understand the concepts of number and time as an indication of talent in this area.

The good news about early childhood programs of all kinds, is that academic skills are only one area of developing potential and no particular pressures are going to be applied to pre-schoolers.

CLAP-
CLAP

What are these strange things my child brings home?

Naturally, all children are proud of the things they produce at pre-school or at school, but for many talented children the question of how something was made rather than what was made is more important. Ask your child how he/she made, say, the collage that has been brought home. The responses can often give you an insight into the thought processes that led to a product. Gifted children think creatively and can see wider implications or symbolism where it is not so obvious to us. Small aspects such as the choice of a particular colour in a painting can be important. Don't forget to display products brought home. All children love seeing their works up on their bedroom wall, in the kitchen or on the side of the refrigerator.

All children love seeing their works up on their bedroom wall, in the kitchen or on the side of the refrigerator.

I have already mentioned it, but remember to ask your child what happened during the day. Don't be surprised if the answer doesn't come until bedtime. This is often the best time to discuss things.

How important is time together?

Times to talk and listen actively are precious, especially for children who will follow through ideas in an unexpected or creative manner. For example, a four-year-old who, on being read *The Bunyip of Berkley's Creek*, wanted to know how the bunyip could talk if he didn't exist! You don't have to know all the answers; just listening to questions will keep the art of questioning alive. 'Time to listen' allows many puzzles and anxieties to emerge and be settled: 'I ate a nice piece of fish tonight, but how did the fish feel?' opens up a dimension of moral questioning.

When asking questions, try to get into the habit of asking 'open questions'. These will help keep your child's brain working. A closed question is 'Would you like to walk around on your hands?' This will usually elicit a yes/no response. An open question is 'How would it be if we all walked around on our hands?' Joan Dalton's book *Adventures in Thinking* and Marilyn Burns' *The Book of Think* are goldmines of information on questioning talented children.

Times to talk and listen actively are precious.

Ask open questions. These will help keep your child's brain working.

Emotional Development

Often parents are worried about young talented children after hearing frightening stories about emotional problems arising in older children. Very little research has been undertaken into how the talented pre-schooler differs emotionally from the non-talented one, but some evidence indicates that talented pre-schoolers feel higher self-esteem, a greater need to achieve and possibly more fear.

Young children see themselves through the eyes of the adults around them.

Young children see themselves through the eyes of the adults around them. Positive feedback by parents and teachers rubs off and is the best insurance that the child will feel valued and 'special'.

Perfectionism may well come from the parent. It is easy to praise performance rather than effort. Parents need to try and promote a delight in trying difficult tasks, but don't expect perfection all the time.

Age 3–5 typically brings fears arising from greater knowledge of the world. Intellectually gifted children are better able to imagine and state their fears; they are also bright enough to begin to grapple with huge problems like God and Nature. Parents can best cope with these by being willing to discuss things openly.

Talented pre-schoolers have been shown to have more energy, enthusiasm and curiosity than non-talented pre-schoolers. Parents can encourage their child's curiosity by answering endless questions and providing opportunities for further exploration.

Social Development

This can be a worry to parents. Intellectually advanced children often have more ideas about how to solve social problems and act co-operatively but these ideas may not be acted upon. They are still small children and have not the experience to see the possible implications of their 'solutions'.

The peer group still largely determines the development of social skills. This is very important when it comes to choosing a pre-school. Parents who value independence choose one kind of pre-school while parents who value co-operation and warmth will choose another. Before school, joining in the neighbourhood play group is important — a mixed age group can be especially useful for the early foundation of social skills.

Value each child as a unique and special individual.

Research indicates there may be problems between talented and non-talented siblings, especially related to the order of birth and sex. Parents need to feel their way and work out methods of minimising conflict. Value each child as unique and special.

5
PARENTS AND SCHOOLS

What Can Schools Do for Talented Children?

Once a child reaches school age, parents must make many decisions and consider a number of factors, such as:

☆ whether the school chosen should be neighbourhood, regional, selective, state, independent, day school or residential;

☆ what options each school offers in terms of curriculum — the range of subjects available, especially extras like music, dancing, art;

☆ what sort of social factors are operating such as geographical distance from home and the peer group at the school;

☆ what attitude is taken by a particular school towards talented children. Some schools pretend such children don't exist, while others have specific programs and a well-developed consistent approach.

Once a child reaches school age, parents make many decisions.

For a detailed picture of what is going on in your state schools, see Eddie Braggart's book, *Education of Gifted and Talented Children: Australian Provision*, obtainable from Australian Government Bookshops or from the Schools Commission in Canberra.

Various curricula are offered by independent schools across Australia. If you are interested in finding out what is available, I suggest you contact your state Independent Schools' Association, listed in the resources chapter at the end of this book, or write to each school individually. Here, I will limit discussion to the most common administrative arrangements and curriculum provision for the talented within the public education system.

AS A PARENT YOU CAN . . .

Make the school aware of any talents your child may have.

Monitor your child's progress, keeping a written record if you like.

Use support services within and outside the school.

Supplement and extend classroom activities with music, ballet and art, for example.

As an education consumer, you should ask your school what is being done to meet the needs of your talented child. If you have the time, you may wish to offer your services or expertise to participate in a program in school hours or out-of-hours. Even offering to transport children to a venue outside the school is greatly appreciated.

Graded Classes

Some schools have graded or 'streamed' classes, where children are grouped together according to criteria such as performance in standardised tests or school-based assessment and examinations. There are many pros and cons for such an arrangement. It aims to have all the children of ability in a particular subject together so that work can be pitched at their level and they can 'spark off' each other.

The main issue of contention centres around accusations of elitism and that some children will be missed in the initial screening process. If schools are flexible and teachers alert, children can move into 'top' classes when their ability is recognised. The problem of 'elitism' is more complex — an egalitarian, democratic society may have a built-in resistance to recognising excellence. Yet we have recognised problems at the other end of the educational scale and solutions are being found to meet these problems. All levels of achievement and ability need to be encouraged and appreciated.

Vertical Streaming

Many schools have vertically streamed classes in some subjects. Here, children are included in a class according to ability in a subject rather than age. Thus the talented mathematicians from Years 4, 5 and 6 might follow a specially devised maths program as a single group. While vertical streaming requires special organisation, it is a very valid option for smaller schools and central schools.

Programmed Material

Some teachers offer programmed material so that children can learn at their own pace. The advantage for schools is that talented children are not removed from the social contact of the regular classroom and the stimulus the talented children can offer is not lost. A variation is to offer specialist extension work for talented

Ask your school what is being done to meet the needs of the talented?

Vertical streaming is a very valid option.

children when they have completed their basic work — usually much sooner than the others.

The main problem with programmed material is that it is usually highly structured in small steps, but talented children take giant steps. Programmed materials also rarely incorporate open-ended questions to stimulate higher level thinking skills. Pace is accelerated, but conceptual levels are not.

Grade-skipping

Grade-skipping has fallen out of favour.

Grade-skipping has fallen out of favour recently. The advantages it offers are that the stimulus talented children bring is not removed, they are less bored, pressure on the class teacher is removed and it is relatively easy to implement.

The disadvantages, however, seem to outweigh the advantages. Social and emotional maturity may not match intellectual maturity; gaps in learning may occur, as programs in higher classes may be aimed at older children rather than at the more talented. As most talented children are talented in a specific area, to skip a grade may lead to difficulties in weaker areas.

Clusters

Groups of schools may get together to organise special activities or 'clusters', in which expertise and resources can be shared. Talented children from three or four nearby schools can travel regularly to attend camps or special classes.

The advantages are obvious. Disadvantages may include transporting the children to and from school, and co-ordinating the programs of three or four schools so that children are not overburdened with conflicting homework demands.

Activity Afternoons

A common arrangement, especially in primary schools, is the organisation of an 'activity afternoon' on a regular basis. One or two afternoons a week are set aside to allow children to follow programs or courses based on their own interests. Children may stay in one or two activities all year or try many activities, thereby widening their experience and encouraging any latent talent. This kind of arrangement allows all children, regardless of ability, to follow an interest or, perhaps, a remedial program.

Specialist Programs

A variation of the activity afternoon is the specialist program. A group of children with similar talent in areas such as writing, computers, maths or art, work with an outside 'expert' each week. This experience can extend and enrich particular abilities. Such programs often operate across year levels, as children are selected on the basis of talent, not age.

There have been many successful programs run for a short time where talented children work in a highly concentrated way. Weekend enrichment camps fall into this category. Such courses in school may take only a month or a term.

An outside person is usually brought in to conduct courses, for example, on public speaking. Music is another area which is taught particularly effectively in this way. Music camps may introduce children to new instruments or provide the chance to work with other enthusiasts in a group.

Clubs and Competitions

A popular way of helping talented children is to form clubs within the school. Clubs which cater for interest in computers are very common, but clubs can be formed to encourage any area of interest. It takes only an enthusiastic teacher, parent or community member with time available to start a club. Many schools also encourage their talented children to participate in competitions, such as public speaking and debating, which are usually organised by Departments of Education. Some private companies, community organisations and tertiary institutions offer competitions in maths, computers, writing, art and photography. Ask your school for information on these competitions or look for announcements in the papers.

Selective Schools

Frequently, I am asked to comment on the pros and cons of special schools and special classes. Special schools for the gifted and talented — opportunity classes (OC) as they are called in New South Wales, for primary students, and selective high schools for secondary students — are not being expanded at the moment. In New South Wales there are about seven selective high schools and only one new school, for the performing arts at Newtown in Sydney, has been created in recent times. A few schools have OC classes for talented children but these are outside the mainstream policy of the Education Department.

The main argument for selective high schools and OC schools and/or classes is that they can cater better for the needs of talented children. Resources can be better employed to meet the intellectual needs of the students; and since the school is composed entirely of talented students, they are working with others of similar abilities all day, every day. These schools can then produce relevant curricula and greater opportunities for extension and enrichment.

Arguments against selective schools have, in recent years, had considerable influence on Education Department policies. Many children selected for such schools may have only one outstanding talent but are average or quite weak in others, which presents problems for the child and for the schools. Children may also be pressured into studying subjects in which they have no interest.

Another problem can arise when teachers with skills to teach the talented are not appointed to selective schools. In New South Wales, teachers are appointed in the same way they would be to a local school. Thus, you can get both good and poor teachers at a selective school in the same way that you can in every other school — state or independent. This, again, depends on how inflexibly a selective schools program is administered.

Some types of social interaction may be absent without the mix of students from all classes and of all abilities. Today's talented children may become the leaders in our community in the future. To fulfil this role successfully, the talented might benefit from an understanding of those less talented than themselves.

Finally, selective schools cater for only a very small number of talented children while, for example, the needs of many children such as those in the country or in isolated areas are not being met. There never is enough money to spend on education, and while funds are limited, local schools may meet more community needs.

The Best Possible Education

Ultimately, you as a parent are faced with the decision about the best possible education for your child. If you feel the local school is inadequate to meet your child's needs, you might consider independent schools which may offer scholarships, specialisation in particular areas, special programs for the Montessori kindergartens and so forth. The choice is yours and needs to be based on a good understanding both of your particular talented child and of what each education system offers.

Whatever the system, we certainly need teachers with the trained skills of teaching talented students. Government and parents need to provide more resources and materials for local schools. Changes in policy can only come with active lobbying from parents and teachers so that all children can be taught at the appropriate level to achieve their full potential.

PROBLEMS AT SCHOOL

Bored with work that is not challenging enough.

Resentment at being interrupted during a lengthy explanation.

Disruption and disrespect for authority and tradition which they may question.

Difficulty in performing group tasks.

Difficulty in coping with conformity. Often teachers think these children are 'going off the subject' as they pursue wide solutions to problems or areas of interest.

They may be penalised for not following directions or meeting deadlines, as such behaviour may be considered rebellious.

Refusal to take part in activities in which they are not interested; or they might not excel; or products are demanded as proof of learning.

Pursuit of other activities before a set task has been completed.

Co-operation and trust are essential.

Co-operating with the School

If the education of talented children is achieved through a good relationship between home and school, the rewards can be enormous for all. Co-operation and trust are essential.

As a parent, you can help the school at the same time as helping your child, by taking an active interest in the school itself. This acts as a model for your child's own behaviour. American research on underachievement has found that many teenage underachievers learnt their negative attitudes from parents with little or no interest in the school.

Your interest can be at the simple level of supporting the Parents and Citizens Association or its local equivalent, or by going to meetings and supporting fund-raising activities. Any expression of interest is an investment in the future, for your child and for other children. It may also help school staff to see you in a more positive light, and to become more familiar with your entire family.

Perhaps you have some special expertise or deep interest that you could offer to the school. Here are two examples. I know a newspaper editor who gives a couple of hours a week to conduct courses in journalism for talented writers in Years 9 and 10. The courses are held after school. Students are selected to attend from both the state high school and the non-state high school. In another case, a retired school principal takes a local primary school's choir and band for practice once a week. Both these people offer skills which would otherwise be unavailable and which may be of great value to the students both now and later.

Schools are usually only too pleased to accept help from such volunteers. As education and society become more complex, teachers simply do not have all of the skills needed. Your commitment may be a ten week semester or once a week all year for an hour or so. It depends on you and the school but it is well worthwhile. Parents in this position always report the value and the pleasure of the experience for themselves and for the children with whom they work.

School-based parent involvement programs cannot, however, ignore the working life of parents. In many cases, it may not be easy for parents to take part within school hours. Single parents may also lack funds for baby sitting while up at the school and may well suffer, as they don't wish to be seen as uncaring or uninvolved.

These problems and any others, can always be discussed with the teacher, the principal and the school counsellor, perhaps out of school hours by appointment. School counsellors in particular have a great deal of experience dealing with social difficulties, and work to establish good relations between parents, children and teachers.

The Mentor Program

Another interesting option is the Mentor Program. One such program in Melbourne began in July 1983 and has reached a stage where there are about 200 mentors and students involved in 'shared learning experiences'.

The program aims to foster individual talent for students whose abilities are not otherwise catered for, by establishing informal long-term relationships with a person willing to share knowledge, skills and experience on a one-to-one basis. The program operates outside school hours at mutually convenient times, through correspondence or 'talking' through a computer. At regular intervals, mentors, organisers and students meet to discuss problems and analyse progress.

The mentor is not a teacher but a specialised guide: an 'encourager' with whom the student can share an interest or talent. Students are nominated in several ways: by themselves, their parents, the school, the teacher or the community. The matching of mentor and student, the organisation, liaising with parents and mentors and so on is done through a task force. This group controls the system and an independent person is available to sort out any problems that arise if the mentor and student are incompatible. Parents have the right to withdraw their child from the program at any time.

I believe such a program has enormous possibilities in catering for the needs of talented children. Mentors obtain a great deal of pleasure working with a talented child who shares a common interest or has a comparable ability, while the child can expand and enrich his/her experience in an area of talent or interest.

Talented Handicapped Children

Government policy in Australia is to integrate handicapped students into the normal stream of education and later into the workforce.

Disabled children with talent must be given every encouragement at home and at school in exactly the same way as talented children without a handicapping condition.

While there are several special schools in Australia established specifically for handicapped children, none as yet has specialised in handicapped talented children. This may well be an area for expansion in the future. Meanwhile, handicapped children should be encouraged to take advantage of any of the talent enrichment programs your school offers.

When Things Go Wrong

Sometimes parents feel that the school does not 'seem to be doing enough' for their child. On the other hand, school principals often ask me as a consultant to have a chat with parents who seem to be 'pushing their kid too hard'. Sometimes there are grounds for grievances, but in most case a rational solution can be reached through co-operation and intelligent communication. Home and school must each know what the other is doing for the talented children, so they can try to reinforce each other's efforts.

Sometimes parents and teachers are surprised to find that they share common objectives. The difficulty is that each is approaching these objectives from different sides. It gets back to sensible, rational communication.

If there is a problem, then a pre-arranged interview is better for all. Both parties can prepare questions which are more likely to result in productive discussion.

The best set of hints and clues for this situation that I have found is from the South Australian Association for Gifted and Talented Children. I thank the association for allowing me to use its ideas which I have expanded upon.

How to Prepare for an Interview

Discuss problems

Discuss school problems thoroughly with your child. You need details in order to raise specific questions with the teacher. Remember, however, that the child is only giving a version from one point of view. Also, your child is only human. If he/she has

a lively imagination and likes to embellish stories for effect (most kids do — so do adults!) then you may want to take with a tiny pinch of salt some of the stories about school. Some horrendous parent-teacher misunderstandings have arisen through a child's desire for attention.

The child is only giving one point of view.

Be specific

If you are convinced there is a real problem at school, do not hesitate to intervene carefully and sensitively.

Keep the issues clear in your own mind. It is not your ego at stake, it's the most appropriate educational program for your child that you are striving for. Before calling the teacher, think through what it is you're concerned about and what you want to ask. Writing out some questions or statements may be helpful; you and the teacher will both need specific examples of problem areas, not merely vague impressions.

Establish good relations with the teacher

Don't criticise or downgrade a teacher in front of your child. The teacher needs authority and respect from the child, and the child does not need the problem of divided loyalties.

Never try to set up a pressure group against a teacher with other parents. Of course the teacher will hear about it and naturally be on the defensive. The problem is the responsibility of you and the teacher; it should not become a public scandal.

Keep in mind that, unless proven otherwise, you and the teacher are probably concerned with the same basic goal — helping your child.

Be courteous

There may be legitimate, honest differences of opinion and judgment about how children should be educated and handled. It might be good to set down for yourself the basic assumptions and beliefs you hold.

If you wish to discuss these, dropping in during class is never satisfactory; you may come during a lesson which cannot be interrupted and then you both feel embarrassed and awkward. Besides, phoning to make an appointment is a basic courtesy, which opens the way for mutually fruitful discussions.

Conducting the Interview

Communicate

Be what you are — a responsible, mature, concerned parent with some questions to present candidly. There is no need to be aggressive and demanding or apologetic, embarrassed, uncomfortable.

Be prepared to listen and ask for explanations when you don't understand. Teachers sometimes lapse into teaching jargon. Don't be afraid to say, 'Look, I'm not sure what you mean by...'. Ask questions to clarify what actually happens in the classroom and express your willingness to help and share in solving the problem.

Use evidence

Emphasise the child's work, feelings, concerns or behaviour. Deal with evidence of the child's actual reaction. In other words, use 'I' rather than 'you' statements: 'I've been talking to Sally and I have some questions about the books she is reading in her class', rather than 'You are giving Sally readers that are too easy for her'. Focus on how the problem can be solved rather than on polarised attitudes such as 'us versus the school' or 'Sally versus the school'.

There may be legitimate, honest differences of opinion about how children should be educated and handled.

Be positive

Be alert for opportunities to be positive about the child and the teacher. Don't dwell on past angers, hurts or complaints and try not to criticise past teachers to your child's present teacher. As well as putting him or her in an impossible professional position, the teacher is going to wonder if you will make the same sort of criticisms to next year's teacher. This is not a foundation for trust!

Don't criticise the teacher personally. Do your best to ensure that neither of you feels defensive or hostile, and be prepared to share with the teacher constructive information about your child's interests and activities outside school.

Ask for specific information

Avoid vague opinions or fuzzy generalisations. See that the discussion focuses on specific areas. If reference is made to tests or test scores ask for a full explanation of the meaning of the scores — numbers aren't useful in themselves. For example, if the teacher says, 'Sally only scored 11 out of 20 in the last maths test' you could ask what are the areas in which she is finding difficulty, what was the content of the test and how did the score of 11 compare with the scores of classmates.

Now what?

By now you have probably reached a solution to your problem that is satisfactory to the child, to you and to the teacher. There may be times, however, when this level of co-operation does not achieve a mutually acceptable result. What do you do next?

If You Still Have a Problem . . .

Don't blow it!

If you feel dissatisfied or uncertain, don't threaten or get angry. Say politely that you are still worried and ask the teacher what else might resolve or clarify the situation. If he/she doesn't know, say that you would like to discuss the matter further with other people, the principal, school counsellor or guidance officer.

Monitor Progress

Go along with a suggestion if it sounds reasonable, and set up another appointment to evaluate the progress. Keep in mind what you and the teacher have agreed upon: what is the teacher going to do? Is he/she doing it? Is anyone else to be involved? What are you going to do? Are you doing it? What is the child expected to do?

Try not to criticise past teachers — the present teacher will wonder if you will make the same sort of criticisms to next year's teacher.

Be encouraging

Encourage the child to accept that everyone must sometimes do things under pressure from others. Help to plan ways in which your child can demonstrate his/her competence in the classroom without being seen as a show-off.

Outside mediators

You may need to seek help within the system, but outside the school. Most education systems have someone from whom you can seek advice or maybe mediation: the district school counsellor, school inspectors or gifted and talented child consultants. Their job is to help children, parents and teachers. I have often found that unpleasant parent-teacher confrontations over talented children could have been avoided if parents had known whom to consult. Sometimes you need a second opinion, just as you might with a medical problem.

Changing Schools

If, despite all efforts, frustration continues, then you may think seriously about finding another school which may be more appropriate for your child's particular needs. Be careful and bear in mind that your child may have made firm friends; the social dislocation may outweigh other considerations. Discuss this possibility thoroughly with your child before taking drastic action.

6
UNDER-
ACHIEVEMENT

What Is Underachievement?

Very few people work to capacity but some children with considerable academic ability fail at subjects in which they should succeed.

When I first became a teacher, I thought that underachievement was a simple thing. My colleagues felt the same. This is why you often see on school reports those dreaded words, 'Not working to potential', or worse still, 'Lazy'. Then I began to wonder why many bright kids didn't work to their recognised potential ability.

Underachievement is more complicated than it at first seems.

As I read more about underachievement among talented children, I discovered that the problem was more complicated than it had first seemed. It is only partly understood and is certainly a matter of great concern for parents and teachers.

One of the best books on the topic, by Jane Raph and others, is *Bright Underachievers*. This book pinpoints the basic problem: what criteria do you use to measure underachievement — school tests, objective standardised test performances or behaviour at school? We all have an image of what it is, but we cannot precisely define it. We can say that it is a grievous waste of talent that prevents the child from having a sense of fulfilment and is a loss to society as a whole.

How It Shows

Two types of underachievement have been identified. The first is where children only achieve on occasions, apparently when the mood takes them. More likely, their refusal to work or put themselves forward for selection in a team can be linked with some emotional crisis that suddenly erupts: a relationship may break up; a family problem may arise; a personality clash may develop with a specific teacher. Generally, these children have few long-term problems if they can get immediate help to overcome their difficulty and their progress at school is closely monitored. These children are known as situational underachievers.

80 per cent of identified underachievers are boys.

The second type of underachiever is a much more serious problem for the school, the home and particularly for themselves. The chronic underachiever has many characteristics that give him a label hard to remove. I use 'him' deliberately, because over 80 per cent of identified underachievers are boys! They may become aggressive, giving vent to their frustration by causing trouble or they may become sulky and withdrawn and refuse to develop their talent.

Many underachieving girls have fallen victim to the expectations of society and of their families. Stereotyping roles for girls can lead to their being forced away from areas in which they have talent or a deep interest, into conventionally female areas. Fortunately this is becoming a thing of the past, as far as schools are concerned, with the implementation of non-sexist education policies. Social change, however, takes time.

Many underachieving girls have fallen victim to expectations of society and their families.

Common Characteristics of Underachievers

The following list is based on Barbara Clark's excellent book *Growing Up Gifted*. Underachievers may:

☆ have a low self-image, often displaying distrust, indifference, lack of concern and/or hostility;

☆ feel rejected by their family and resist attempts to help by parents or teachers;

☆ feel victimised or helpless and may not accept any responsibility for themselves or their actions;

☆ choose friends with similar negative attitudes to school, show no leadership qualities and may be less mature than their peers;

☆ have little motivation with poor study habits; may refuse to do homework or leave much work incomplete;

☆ are often impulsive with poor personal judgement and adjustment abilities;

☆ have poor test results at school and no hobbies or interests at home;

☆ either cannot plan for the future or set goals well below their true ability or potential.

Very depressing! But familiar to many readers both as parents and as teachers. All teachers, especially in high school, will have encountered such children in their class at one time or another.

Causes of Underachievement

Experts are divided on the causes of underachievement. There has been little research in Australia; most information is based on research in urban schools in the United States. There may be regional differences but one thing is outstandingly clear: underachievers are made and not born. It is the child's choice to underachieve. Like everything else we have discussed in this book, we have to look at both sides of the educational coin: the school and the home.

I believe the American research, such as that carried out by Jane Raph and her associates, underestimates the importance of peer pressure on talented children. It may be one social cause of underachievement where the Australian picture differs from the American. The pressure on children, especially at high school, to conform to the mediocre often has more influence than anything parents or teachers can say. 'Intelligent' boys will be seen as snobbish, sissy, weak or lacking the necessary machismo to get on in our sports-oriented society. Footballers and cricketers are hailed as gods in the media. When was the last time you saw a young man being praised for his achievements as a writer or painter? 'Intelligent guys don't pull the birds!' The academic boy may perceive himself as being unattractive to girls. He may think that girls would rather be seen with the school sporting hero than a keen scholar.

Underachievers are made and not born. It is the child's choice to underachieve.

For girls there has been a conditioning and stereotyping to accept a lesser role in society. For a very long time, less importance was attached to girls' education. Girls were expected to be interested in the arts and humanities but not in more scientific subjects. Some girls don't want to appear too intelligent in case they don't attract the 'best' boys. For the average teenage girl trying to find her way through the jungle of puberty and maturation, intelligence can be unwanted baggage.

Fortunately there is a silver lining. Negative peer pressure is generally a passing phase. As the pressure to succeed at the Higher School Certificate increases, so too does the realisation that one way to a happy and successful future is to work hard to obtain a particular job or to gain a place at university or college.

Another cause of underachievement can be family background. Many children come from a home environment that devalues education. I have met families who deliberately demean schools and teachers in front of their gifted children. Also there can be difficulties when some members of the family perceive a bright child is showing off.

If a family is frequently on the move, for one reason or another, it can mean that the children are never in a school long enough for any talent to be recognised, let alone developed and nurtured. It's quite possible for people with the potential to do exceptionally well, to go through life without realising that they have a gift which can, and should, be developed.

American research considers the major cause of underachievement among the talented to be emotional disturbance between parent and child. Children like this are angry at the parents for some reason and vent their anger and frustration in many ways. They feel they must hurt their parents by failing at school and not allowing them to take pride in their achievements. There are probably five main reasons for this conflict.

1. Conflict between the parents when one parent (often the father) is a perfectionist and the other tries to compensate for this. The child starts to achieve to please dad, but then feels pressure from mum which carries the message: 'You don't need to work so hard!' The child becomes confused trying to please both parents.
2. Sometimes the family has unrealistic, perfectionist expectations and the child equates his/her own worth with doing well at school rather than simply being an individual.
3. A very common situation is a negative relationship with a father who feels threatened by his son surpassing him and being more successful at school than he was.

For a teenage girl, intelligence can be unwanted baggage.

A child can become confused trying to please both parents.

4. Another common problem is a parent who believes that he or she is encouraging the child, but who always wants more than the child does. With the best of intentions, the parent is sending out messages that the child cannot think well enough on his own. As a result, the child learns not to trust his own judgement.

5. Some parents are 'pushy' and try to relive their own lives through their children and force them along at too fast a pace, causing stress and unhappiness. Such pushy parents cannot accept that their children are only children. The child's only defence is to deliberately fail at school. A vicious circle like this can only be broken if the parents learn to understand what is happening.

Any of these problems is likely to create a poor self-image. Fearing success so much, the child creates failure. Such a child prefers not to complete work rather than be awarded a grade that he or she feels will not reach the parents' expectations.

What Can You, as a Parent, Do?

Keep in mind that chronic underachievement will not be solved quickly in a week, a month or even a year. It will take time, patience and co-operation. You will feel frustrated, sometimes angry, but you must persevere. Ask yourself these questions.

Some parents try to relive their own lives through their children.

☆ Have I given my child the impression that I want him or her to achieve to please me?

☆ Have I placed too much emphasis on the importance of accomplishments instead of caring for him/her?

☆ Do I react badly if my child doesn't do well or is uninterested in things I want him/her to be interested in?

☆ Do I undermine my child's confidence, making him/her feel guilty as he/she becomes older and more independent?

☆ How do I react when my child feels angry? Do I use sarcasm or emphasise those things he/she may not yet be good at?

☆ Do I set an appropriate role model myself?

Answering these questions may put the relationship between you and your child into a balanced perspective.

What to Avoid

Never take away the thing or things that a child loves and succeeds in. This may be piano, sport, play or some other leisure activity. To say that a child can't do this until there has been some improvement at school is a sure recipe for disaster, and the resulting sense of deprivation and frustration will lead to even less achievement.

Don't lecture or nag a child. Reason is always preferable. Saying things like, 'You have brains, why don't you use them?' reinforces feelings of inadequacy.

Don't pressure the child into doing something because you think it's a good idea. At a talented child enrichment weekend, I met a very unhappy boy who was 'doing computers' because his mother thought it would be better for him. He wanted desperately to participate in the drama program!

Don't set artificial times for work to be done at all costs and make the child feel that you are being a martyr. This reinforces the idea of failure, not only at school but at home as well. Be more natural in your interest and enthusiasm.

Finally, don't keep checking up on the child's progress. This seems to the child that he or she is irresponsible and not in control of life. It also implies a damaging lack of trust.

What to Do

Once you have found the cause of the problem, the earlier a new approach starts the more effective it will be.

It is essential to build the child's self-confidence and independence. A few simple things about the house can do wonders. Let the child make real decisions and live with the consequences. You may wish to guide, but allow the child to make the final decision. Let your child decide how to manage his/her pocket money, choose their own lunch or decide what to wear. The child may make mistakes but that's how people learn. Encourage the child to see him or herself as a unique individual with a valuable contribution to make to the family and society.

Learn to trust the child's judgement.

Learn to trust the child's judgement. A talented child will at some point make the right decision on problems which have to be faced. Often the child is learning about life. Sidney Parnes' 'Creative Problem Solving' strategy will give you a good insight into how bright kids can work through problems. (See Noller, Parnes, and Biendi, *Creative Action Book*, listed in the resources chapter.)

Get used to saying things which make it clear that the child's feelings are important and that you value his or her opinions. Explain that it's all right to feel angry but that it must be expressed in acceptable ways. Your relationship with your child must be based on mutual respect.

Your relationship with your child must be based on mutual respect.

It often helps an underachieving child to point out achievable goals for them. Put the goals in some priority order, but be flexible. Guide, don't push.

Negative peer group pressure may be counteracted with gently persuasive arguments that point to the adult advantages, financial and social, that come after doing well at school. Point out that a good school reference can get you a good job which in turn can give the adult later on, a car and money, independence and self-respect.

How Schools Can Help

Schools must try to provide help for underachieving children. Children will not turn into achievers overnight; it takes time and careful planning of an integrated program across the curriculum. Children who are underachieving should be allowed to study the basics through areas of interest of expertise. At all stages the parents should be involved. If both parents work, it is still possible to form an effective partnership between home and school by communicating after hours.

Teachers and administrators can show they value the achievements of high ability students by publicising those achievements in school magazines, in assemblies and in the community through the media.

It is a good idea for schools to establish a system of student profiles that should show the first signs of underachievement or

difficulties in talented children. Remedial work should quickly follow. If underachievement becomes too frequent, it's time for the school to evaluate its programs and develop the teachers professionally.

It helps if schools have a learning environment that is flexible, open, accepting and challenging for all students. Give underachievers the opportunity to work at their area of ability and make sure someone the child respects is available when help is needed. Isolation is a fine fertiliser for underachievement.

Isolation is a fine fertiliser for underachievement.

Parental involvement should be encouraged. It is important to arrange sessions with the children and their parents. Involve parents in all school activities. Let them know what is going on at the school. Contact them immediately anything appears to be going wrong.

If a school can offer career and vocational guidance as early as possible, children have the opportunity to establish goals and so have a much greater chance of fulfilling their potential.

7
TWENTY QUESTIONS
— AND THEIR
ANSWERS

What are IQ tests?

There are two types of intelligence quotient (IQ) tests — group and individual. Group tests are most commonly used in schools because they're comparatively simple to carry out and interpret. Traditionally, they have been given in Years 4 and 6 to groups of children. Sometimes individual tests are given, usually by the school counsellor. These tests are considered more accurate.

The Stanford-Binet Intelligence Scale is sometimes used. It was developed to test general intellectual ability including vocabulary and understanding of language, memory evaluation, conceptual and abstract thinking, reasoning ability, manual dexterity and social maturity and judgement — all in 60 to 90 minutes. It was never based on an exact definition of intelligence but rather on relative performance.

Like most similar tests, the Stanford-Binet gives the result as an IQ. This is worked out by dividing mental age — as discovered on the test — by chronological age, times one hundred. Average IQ is standardised at 100, with the middle 50 per cent of the population falling between 90 and 100 IQ.

Another common IQ test sometimes used in schools is the WISC-R (Weschler Intelligence Scale for Children — Revised).

Despite recent questioning of the validity of IQ tests as the sole indicator of intelligence, they can still be useful. However, they should not be the only identification device used.

Is it harmful for children to read and write early?

No! Many children are 'spontaneous' readers and writers and this can be delightful for both you and your child. The spontaneity, by the way, is probably the result of the child's own ability together with the impetus you have provided by showing him or her books, by reading and by answering questions when the child is still very young. Preventing children from reading at an early age is as bad as trying to force them to read before they are ready or capable.

About 50 per cent of talented children can read before they go into kindergarten. If your child can read, tell the school when you enrol your child. This will alert teachers that reading readiness activities will not be necessary, and that reading basic books will be of little use and may bore your child.

Reading, of course, means understanding, not merely sounding out words. Both you and your child's teacher should ensure that the child understands what he or she is reading. A child who makes 'educated guesses' at unknown words, predicts what might come next or self-corrects is probably reading in my sense.

Reading means understanding, not merely sounding out words. Ensure that your child understands what he or she is reading.

Is television harmful for talented children?

I must confess I've changed my views on the subject. For many years I considered that television was of little benefit to bright children. I thought it stifled conversation and took away imagination and innocence. I still hold these views, though with less conviction. In my work I have seen talented children from homes where there is no television. I have seen those whose viewing is strictly controlled by the parents. At the other extreme, I have come across very talented children who are allowed to watch what they like.

Some talented children use television as a learning experience. Many pre-school readers have the multiple elements of written language, oral language and image to help them read. 'Sesame Street' is a good example of this. Talented children soon become discriminating television viewers. They will either watch programs for information or else use the medium to help them relax. (Hence some bright children will watch what we adults consider to be absolute rubbish.)

I don't think a little television does any harm. Be wary of the child who simply sits in front of the television and watches anything and everything just because it is on. Actively discourage this, and encourage children to make choices.

Some talented children use television as a learning experience and become discriminating viewers.

My ten-year-old has poor physical co-ordination and does not enjoy sport and games, but thinks and dreams computers. Should we invest in a computer at home?

Yes! Any deep, long-standing interest should be encouraged. A home PC is something the whole family can use and enjoy. I would be inclined to encourage the child to use the computer for more practical activities as well as for recreational use. Don't let the computer become the be-all and end-all of the child's life to the exclusion of all other interests and activities. Computers can become very addictive!

Fields of interest can be widened via the computer.

Fields of interest can be widened via the computer. Reading can be encouraged by giving access to magazines and books about computers. Not only material on the use of computers, but information on the history and development of computers and mathematics could also be made available. Stories written on a word processor can help improve literacy skills. Family finances and the child's personal finances can be kept on a database. There are obvious links between computers and extending the mathematical skills of a talented child. Joining the computer club at school or a community computer users' group will bring the child into contact with people of similar interests.

Responsibility can be encouraged if the young computer whiz has to save up and buy his/her own disks or other software, although Mum and Dad might subsidise such activities.

Should I tell my child he/she is talented?

Most talented children know they are different and take it in their stride. Others may feel inferior. Some parents feel shock when told by a teacher that their child is talented: 'I didn't know!' is not an uncommon reaction. Generally, they are, at least inwardly, pleased.

Most talented children know they are different and take it in their stride.

Real difficulty arises only if the child gets big headed. In this case, wise counselling may be necessary to point out that we are all individuals with strengths and weaknesses.

Is there a danger of putting too much pressure on a talented child too soon?

Yes! Allow the talented child to follow his/her own interests. Do not subject them to adult imposed pressures. If they enjoy something, some talented children will put pressure upon themselves which, if controlled, will be enjoyable and challenging and produce the satisfaction of a job well done.

What can I do if my child feels lonely or isolated?

Everyone has times when they feel lonely and isolated. A feeling of self-confidence helps to overcome this. All children need to feel comfortable about themselves and develop self-esteem. A warm family environment, a circle of family friends and perhaps taking part in clubs or hobby groups will all lessen the isolation. If the child's isolation seems extreme, a school counsellor may be able to help him/her find ways to deal with particular problems.

All children need to feel comfortable about themselves and develop self-esteem.

How can I help my child with peer group problems?

Again, clubs and hobby groups may help a child overcome negative peer group pressure by introducing him/her to like-minded children. If the child loses confidence and starts underachieving, consult the school counsellor.

How can I encourage a talented child without hurting the other children?

Encourage, enjoy and develop the individual strengths of each child in your family. Do not emphasise the achievements of one against the lesser achievements of the others. Don't make comparisons within the family as this invites competition and rivalry. Give each child a fair share of love and attention so that all your children feel that they are of value as individuals.

Why do some children fear failure?

Some people will have a go at just about anything while others are afraid of trying something new in case they fail. It's all a matter of the way people think.

If your child is worried about failure, discuss it. Talk about your own failures — the shelves that fell down, the burnt cake, the tent that collapsed in the middle of a wet and windy night. Learn to laugh about such mistakes. Stress that having tried something once, it becomes easier and can end up being quite enjoyable.

Is it bad for my son to daydream?

No! In fact, it is a common and rather endearing characteristic of the talented, a little like the eccentricity some of them show. He is simply 'just thinking'. Take care, however, that he does not daydream in potentially dangerous situations.

Give each child a fair share of love and attention.

If your child is worried about a failure, discuss it.

What can I do about my daughter's gullibility?

This is a characteristic often found in sensitive people. They tend to accept people at face value. The only solution is to gently make them aware that the world is not always as it seems and there may be many unpleasant people about. Programs such as 'Stranger Danger' have done much to show young children that dangers always exist.

Will a special class create bad feeling in a school?

No, not if it is properly planned and taught. Special classes (of any kind) should not be given any more publicity than other classes. So, if there is to be a school display mounted, all children have to participate and have their work displayed. Using the terms 'gifted' and 'talented' to denote a special class is courting trouble. A little competition never hurt anyone, indeed some talented children thrive on it. It is better for schools to foster a spirit of co-operation and joint problem solving.

How can I tell if a school or program is good for my child?

A good school or program should mean that your child will be eager to go to school. Any interests picked up at school will be brought home by the child through enthusiastic discussion and an interest in finding additional information. Any program should extend and/or enrich your child's talents, skills and interests into new and expanded areas.

Special classes should not be given any more publicity than other classes.

Should my child's social, emotional and physical development keep pace with his/her intellectual ability?

Yes, if possible. Sometimes a child's skills develop at different rates but they are all as important as intellectual development. On the other hand, no matter how talented, a child is still a child. Children with reasoning ability well beyond their years, can still have nightmares after watching a monster on television. In fact their sensitivity can make this more likely for them than for an 'average' child.

How can I help with homework?

Homework helps talented children master the skills of independent, unsupervised study. It helps consolidate the day's learning and can give practice at skills which might be difficult to master in a crowded classroom. By supervising homework regularly, parents can keep in touch with the work the child is doing at school and, at the same time, show they are interested in their children's work. As far as possible, parents should provide a regular time and place for homework. Don't nag, however. Parents can lighten the burden of homework by encouraging the child to play in the fresh air when getting home from school. Watching television, listening to the radio or to records for a while won't hurt either, as children need time to relax.

Sometimes parents may feel inadequate to help a child with homework — this is quite common for parents of all children, for example with new mathematics. If you are having problems, the obvious person to consult is the child's teacher, then the school principal and finally, the school counsellor. Alternatively, problems can be discussed with other parents and possibly taken up at your P and C meetings.

What can be done about the over-enthusiastic teacher who tends to overload my child with work?

This seems to be more common in high schools where students have different teachers in different subjects who might not co-

ordinate the amount and type of work given. Discuss it with the principal. Check around to see if other children have similar complaints. The amount of work your child is given should be thoroughly documented before you go to the school, using examples over a fortnight. Don't make a big issue of this as it often embarrasses children. In the majority of cases, the teacher is unaware of the work overload. In my experience, it is solved simply by the heads of the various faculties getting together to make sure their teachers co-ordinate work given to classes.

Do talented children need vocational guidance?
Of course they do! One difficulty is that talented children may have an array of career choices. Sometimes they choose unfulfilling, unchallenging jobs well below their ability. (See the chapter on underachievement).

Career guidance can begin at home long before the child's final year at school. Try and support the child's choice of career, irrespective of financial reward. School work experience programs and specialist careers teachers are often successful in steering children towards suitable careers.

Since talented children may have an array of career choices offer guidance as early as possible.

Will a child maintain his/her talent?
This book stresses that ability must be encouraged for it to flourish and enrich the life of the child. But, no matter what, talent does not disappear, although it may decline in a sterile environment.

Talent does not disappear, although it may decline.

Why is there sometimes hostility towards gifted people?
There is a tendency in human nature to 'cut down tall poppies'. Sometimes people feel suspicious of or threatened by something that is different or not understood.

Conversely, because people relate more easily to others with similar interests and abilities, talented people may find it hard to understand how average people behave and think.

Encouraging tolerance on both sides seems a sensible solution.

8
CASE STUDIES: THE TALENTED IN ACTION

There have been many Australians who have achieved highly in diverse areas of endeavour. Think of the high achievers in fields such as the arts, the sciences, business, sport, entertainment — from historical examples such as W. C. Wentworth and Dame Nellie Melba, to more recent examples like Paul Hogan, Dick Smith, Dame Joan Sutherland and Evonne Cawley.

Fortunately, the brain drain overseas, a feature of past generations, seems to have slowed down considerably. Some Australians are now capable of achieving world-wide success without ever leaving on the first Qantas flight to London or Los Angeles.

In this chapter, I have included a selection of case studies of talented children, to illustrate the world of the talented in action. The vast majority of these children will lead rewarding, fulfilling and happy lives. Like the rest of humanity, there will be some who find life more difficult than others. Given encouragement and support at home, and extension and enrichment at school, these children should grow up into worthy citizens making a valuable contribution to society through their special gifts.

Identifying Talented Children

She would be completely content and absorbed in the world she had created.

Belinda

Belinda, the quiet achiever, received great pleasure as a four-year-old from a piece of wood about 30 cm square, and a piece of cloth about twice that size. Used with her doll's pram, the wood and the cloth became different basic structures that set the scene for whatever kind of game she and her family of toys chose to play that day. Usually the particular game would continue for several hours and she would be completely content and absorbed in the world she had created.

Alison

Remarkable powers of memory may be displayed very early in life. When Alison was 18 months old, she and her mother were in the garden and her mother pointed out a large, brightly coloured caterpillar on a tree trunk. A year later, they were walking in the garden and Alison pointed at an identical caterpillar on the same tree, saying, 'This is like the other one we saw here another time!'

Piet

Piet received 150/100 marks for a mathematics competition because he discovered a new way to solve a maths problem that had not even occurred to the university lecturers who set the question. He now has a PhD in pure and applied mathematics!

Anya

Anya was ten when she arrived at a new school. Very little was known about her or her family, except that her mother had died. Teachers described her work as average and she was well behaved in class. A perceptive teacher intuitively felt that there was more to the girl than first met the eye. Chatting to her over a period of time, the teacher found out that the girl's father worked long shifts in the steel works and the ten-year-old had the responsibility of caring for her four younger brothers and sisters. Not only did she have to wash the youngest, read to them and put them to bed, she cooked all the family's meals and did the housework. The home was immaculate. Her father allowed her to work out the family budget, pay the bills and do the shopping. A talented ten-year-old!

More was to come. Her hobby was doing petitpoint. This was outstanding in its technical execution and creativity. She has since been able to exhibit and sell her work to earn extra money.

Jenny

Jenny, now in Year 11, throughout her school career expressed her feelings openly and in a very forthright way on questions of injustice. Jenny was often asked by the other pupils to present their case when they were in trouble or when the group believed their rights were being disregarded. At high school, she refused election as a prefect because (in her words) 'The system is a lot of rubbish and I can do more for other kids when not bound by the prefect system!'

Johann

Johann developed an almost fanatical interest in a particular series of books on films, collecting them all and cataloguing them as he did with all his books. He kept records of all his book purchases, visits to the cinema, etc. These scrapbooks were kept with infinite care and artistically presented. In high school his interest in films increased and he dealt with a rather unhappy family life (poor relationship with his father) by centring his interests on films and books. There was one particular film for which he developed something of an obsession and he painted a scene from it for his major work in the Higher School Certificate.

He dealt with a rather unhappy family life by centring his interests on films.

When he left school, he wrote to every film distributor to get a job and succeeded in doing so. Initially, his work was to supply the newspapers with information about the films showing each week, and gradually his duties extended to preparing artwork and posters. Within a few years, he was in charge of a film distributor's art department.

Overcoming Problems

Angela

Some neighbours of mine were worried about their child of three and a half, who could read fluently, showed good number concepts and was learning to play the piano. Angela was an only child and very demanding, often waking in the small hours, wanting to play or read. Obviously, the parents had structured the child's learning experiences well and had achieved considerable success.

They became unstuck when the child was given a puzzle for a birthday present and she experienced difficulty in completing it, refusing to consider solutions without dad's help. The incident clearly showed that the child had a lot to learn and should be given opportunities to explore and learn for herself in a less structured way. More time had to be found to do things just for fun! The parents had to become parents rather than teachers.

I urged them to let the child use her own imagination more — childhood is too brief to allow imagination and innocence to wither. Open-ended questions and activities were recommended. I suggested that they do more things together — gardening, going on picnics, shopping, washing the car. All this was informal learning and having fun.

A few months later, Angela was often seen outside the confines of her house and frequently came to play with my children. She was being treated as a child first and a talented child second. The street was filled with the infectious laughter of little children playing!

Time had to be found to do things just for fun. The parents had to become parents rather than teachers.

Maria

Talented children from ethnic backgrounds can present problems for schools wishing to develop their talent. This is especially so for girls.

Maria came from a Greek background. She was the only girl in the family and had three brothers. Her music teacher at high school noticed that she took a great interest in music in Year 7 and took the subject as an elective in Year 8, even though she did not play a musical instrument. Mary excelled at singing and to a lesser extent in folk dancing. Her problem was that she was not allowed to show it at home. This was the role of her brothers. Encouragement from the school met a cultural barrier at home, as family tradition had cemented her into the role that she should not out-shine her brothers.

The school tried to extend and enrich Maria's talent and interest in music through her music lessons. She joined the school choir which was most successful in local competitions. Unfortunately, she was not allowed to travel to Sydney to perform in the Opera House, until a trusted neighbour acted as a chaperone. At least this was a breakthrough. Maria's teacher had to tread softly and not offend her parents. She, the teacher, hoped that as the family stayed longer in Australia, they would more readily accept Australian customs without losing their own identity, and Maria might be given more opportunities to develop her talent.

Primary school case study

As I was writing this book, I was approached by a group of parents who were very concerned that a proposed change in maths teaching at the local primary school might have profound effects on their more able sons and daughters.

For some years, maths teaching in the school had been based on ability grouping. Students were taught at three levels according to their achievements in the subject. All were taught a basic core, while the more able had an extension program, and the less able followed a remedial program based on the core. Everyone was happy until a new executive teacher was appointed to the school. About halfway through the academic year, the hitherto successful system was changed and the whole structure demolished. Unfortunately, two of the brighter children overheard a conversation where the new teacher said he wanted a change because he could not handle the low ability students. This was reported to the parents who noted that this was not the reason given to them for the change in maths program.

My advice, as a consultant, was for them to marshal all their facts, including evidence that the more able were suffering in their maths skills as a result of the change. They then had to make an appointment with the principal to discuss the matter with him. Some of the parents were fearful of approaching the principal, but two of the mothers were actively involved in the school and had found him approachable and co-operative on other matters.

The result was a half hour meeting in a spirit of co-operation based on a common philosophy that the children must come first. The graded maths program was reinstituted, and the three Year 6 teachers rotated among the classes on a regular basis. The teach-

Much can be achieved between schools and parents with the common philosophy that the children must come first.

ing program was based on the children's needs not on the teachers'. The expertise of the staff was better utilised; for example, the new teacher turned out to be a very good teacher of advanced maths which no one knew when he arrived at the school. Another teacher had expertise in remedial maths, but liked the occasional excursion into the world of advanced maths. Everyone was happy!

Coming to Terms with Giftedness

A child's story

'Occasionally teachers seem to be foes rather than allies. If a student happens to learn rapidly or already has a knowledge of the subject from prior experience, such a teacher develops a deep resentment towards him. In my case, I had an algebra teacher who developed this type of resentment. I understood the material, I seldom missed problems on tests, homework or on the board and when I did I caught his wrath. I don't know the psychological reasons. I only know this situation shouldn't exist.

'I have had many difficult experiences because I was able to grasp subject matter quickly. Often a teacher gets so involved with students who learn slowly that he gives 'busy work' to the student who does know. Crossword puzzles and Scrabble just don't seem to satisfy my educational needs! Many teachers ignore the situation completely. Some revert to hostile behaviour. Many teachers resent students who are bright and punish them with remarks in class and poor scores. Consequently the student becomes bitter and often becomes a behaviour problem.

'I've seen this happen many times and yet could do little or nothing. But then finally there was the teacher who acknowledged my 'hunger' for material and provided incentive and true learning experiences. He even could refer me to another teacher or a new method of learning. This is the teacher who provided enough incentive for me to stay in school. At least in my case it did. It is a pity that there are so few teachers like this! One can only hope that experiences like this will become increasingly rare, as parents and teachers both become more aware of how vulnerable and frightened a child, talented or not, can be.'

Story 2 'I just want to be normal'

This story comes from the Training Manual for volunteer Counsellors, published by the Queensland Association for the Gifted and Talented.

'I do not like being labelled G and T (gifted and talented) or bright. I just want to be normal.

'When my friends ask me where I have been and I have been out with the Explorers Club or G and T Association I am embarrassed to explain.

'Some people in the Association and outside of it put expectations on me to perform some "genius feat" to show them I am gifted. If I can't do something which they expect I should, then they say, "If you are supposed to be gifted how come you don't know this or can't do that?"

'I don't think of myself as gifted. It doesn't worry me one way or the other. I am "ME". Other people tell me I have extraordinary ability but I didn't think so for many years. At high school I did start to compare and recognise and feel it myself.

'In primary school I chose not to play many of the "normal" games other children enjoyed because I saw the games as futile and without challenge.

'I could not relate to many of the children because I saw them as babyish. They weren't interested in the intellectual games I enjoyed such as chess, Monopoly, Scrabble, or books on science, space, origami, marine life, aeroplanes. However, sometimes I used to pretend to be dumb or do stupid things to bring myself into my peer group for acceptance.

'At high school, I still find my peers display immature behaviour, are uninteresting, boring people. I have always related better with older kids or adults. Even some adults are boring.

'It would help if teachers tried to become close to the students in the class and become friends so the student does not have to cautiously communicate to the teacher. So he can just talk to the teacher naturally and unfold his problems and difficulties in a natural way. Just telling a teacher that a student is gifted does not necessarily lead to any understanding. Most teachers seem to stay aloof and "teach" and prefer not to get to know the student as an individual.

'Because I am gifted in some subjects, teachers can't seem to accept failure from me in other subjects because I don't see them

'I don't think of myself as gifted. It doesn't worry me one way or the other. I am me!'

as relevant or they are incredibly boring or the teacher is boring in the presentation of the subject. I know I am underachieving but it does not concern me. A pass is good enough. Do I have to achieve to please the teacher? I resent their "put downs" and their expectations.

'My father has always felt threatened by my ability and is always trying to prove he is superior to me. Always competing, he tries to set me up for failure. I have lost a lot of respect for him because he can't accept me. There is more to me than my intellectual ability. It is only a part of me and it is only a part of my life. I realise now as I get older that friendships, a social life and social skills are much more fulfilling and necessary to my life, more than intellectual pursuits.'

'There is a lot more to me than my intellectual ability . . . Friendships, a social life and social skills are much more fulfilling.'

A mother's story

'Suzanne was always calling for attention. She constantly wanted to be held, to see what was going on around her. My friends told me that I was spoiling her but it was the only way to keep her happy. It wasn't until I'd had my second child that I realised Suzanne's behaviour was unusual. My second child was everything that Suzanne wasn't — calm, placid, happy and loving. Suzanne has become more affectionate over the years, but I feel she has learnt this from Julie.

'We talked to her in an adult manner from an early age, I remember reasoning with her when she was eight months old! And it worked! She showed no interest in reading before starting school. She was a loner at kindergarten and at pre-school and still is today at school. She is very sensitive, a frown can bring on the tears. She cannot stand "bad vibrations" at home or at school and becomes upset when a classmate is chastised especially if it is done vocally and loudly.

'The first eighteen months at school were uneventful. Halfway through Grade Two she hated school, it was "boring" and we would have battles each morning as she was made to go to school. My family doctor suggested that I go for help as something was obviously wrong. An unofficial test showed that Suzanne was very bright and after this the whole family relaxed and got on much better. Suzanne told me after the test that she was relieved to know that she was bright, she was worried that she was going mad. There was no one at school like her and that was the only explanation that she could work out for herself. I found this upsetting as I'd always thought that we had a good relationship between us, but even so she hadn't felt that she could talk this over with me.

'My hopes for Suzanne are not grandiose. I'd like her to come to terms with her giftedness and become a happy well-balanced adult. I would like her to use the full extent of the abilities that she possesses, but her wishes must come first.'

'My hopes for Suzanne are not grandiose. Her wishes must come first.'

9
THE FUTURE

Education for excellence, allowing talent to be nourished to its fullest capacity, is an investment in the future. Israel and Sweden have already established models for the education of gifted children.

The people of Israel have a long tradition which places a premium on education as a matter of personal satisfaction, national pride and survival as a nation.

Sweden, a small nation with few natural resources other than its people, has a standard of living that is the envy of most other countries. By encouraging and utilising talent, Sweden is a world leader in the particular fields of industry in which it has chosen to specialise.

In Australia, the future for talented children is better than it has been for decades. Those with educational influence and power are becoming aware of these children and their needs.

All states have policies that make it mandatory for public schools to cater for the needs of the talented. In many schools exciting and innovative programs are in operation or are being planned. Most Education Department regions have a consultant for the education of the talented. Others have a task force or committee to advise and counsel teachers.

Much more needs to be done. This can really only be achieved by active and constructive lobbying. Parents and teachers can apply political pressure by writing letters to the press and to members of Parliament and by joining the state Associations for the Education of Talented Children.

Educating both young and experienced teachers in the needs of the talented is another area requiring expansion. Teacher training institutions must offer more training courses to prepare teachers to teach talented children without being threatened by them.

In time, every school may have access to a specialist teacher for teaching talented children, just as some schools now have resource teachers employed to assist teaching the less able.

Although we have many new avenues still to explore, the education of the talented has now been accepted as a national educational priority. Our children are our future. It is up to us to give Australians the best future we can.

Education for excellence is an investment in the future.

10
WHAT TO DO?
WHERE TO GO?

This chapter contains various recources for obtaining further information about the education of your talented child. Associations for Gifted and Talented Children exist in every State and can be contacted for up-to-date details on books, kits, activities and contact with other families of talented children.

Parents looking for child assessment and advice can refer to the Guidance and Counselling section, which lists a number of organisations in each State. Parents can consult these bodies independently or follow the usual protocol of going through their child's school, via a class teacher, school counsellor or principal.

The section on Special Provision for the Talented in Various States indicates some of the activities provided for talented children within the State school system. Independent schools have varying curricula and can be consulted privately or through the relevant State Association of Independent Schools.

Finally, the Book List provides comprehensive further reading and the section on Kits offers useful resource material readily available to parents.

ASSOCIATIONS FOR GIFTED AND TALENTED CHILDREN

Australian Association for Gifted and Talented
  Children
c/- Dr Ken Imison
Darling Downs Institute of Higher Education
Toowoomba Queensland 4350

New South Wales Association for Gifted and
  Talented Children
PO Box 165
Moorebank 2170
Secretary: telephone (02) 821 2952

ACT Association for Gifted and Talented
  Children
PO Box 99
Lyneham, ACT 2602
Telephone: (062) 48 9036

Victorian Association for Gifted and Talented
  Children
PO Box 184
Glen Waverley 3150
Executive officer: telephone (03) 232 4287

Queensland Association for Gifted and
  Talented Children
PO Box 121
Ashgrove 4060
Telephone: (07) 30 1878

South Australian Association for Gifted and
  Talented Children
1/24 Dover Street
Malvern 5061
Secretary: telephone (08) 272 4537

Northern Territory Association for Gifted and
  Talented Children
Birrimba Station
PMB 72
via Katherine 5780
Telephone: (089) 75 0751

West Australian Association for Gifted and
  Talented Children
Meeralinga House
Hay Street
West Perth 6005

Tasmanian Association for Gifted and
  Talented Children
6 Ellison Street
Newstead 7250
Telephone: (003) 44 8207

GUIDANCE AND COUNSELLING

New South Wales

State Coordinating Committee for the
  Education of the Talented Child
Division of Services
Department of Education
PO Box 439
North Sydney 2060
Chairperson: telephone (02) 923 4372
Executive officer: telephone (02) 923 4571

You can also contact your local regional office
  of the Education Department; the addresses
  are given in the white pages phone book,
  under NSW Government, Department of
  Education.

Regional guidance officers and consultants
School counsellors

Foundation for Child and Youth Studies
University of NSW Professional Suite
Kirkbride Block
Rozelle Hospital
Church Street
Leichhardt 2040
Telephone (02) 810 0601

Assessment of students:
Division of Guidance and Special Education
Regional guidance officers at regional offices of
  Education Department

Equal opportunity issues/education of girls:
Social Development Unit
Office of the Minister of Education
Education Building
35–39 Bridge Street
Sydney 2001
Telephone (02) 240 8476

New South Wales Catholic Education
  Commission
11th Floor, Polding House
276 Pitt Street
Sydney 2000
Telephone (02) 264 7211

Association of Independent Schools of New
  South Wales
Suite 5, 9th Floor, Wynyard House
291 George Street
Sydney 2000
Telephone (02) 29 2175

Tertiary education
New South Wales Office of Higher Education
13th Floor
189 Kent Street
Sydney 2000
Telephone (02) 237 6500

Australian Capital Territory

Equal opportunity issues/education of girls:
Coordinator for the Elimination of Sexism in
  Education
ACT Schools Authority
MacArthur House
Northbourne Avenue
Lyneham 2602
Telephone (062) 49 0211

ACT Diocesan Catholic Education Office
Archdiocese Canberra-Goulburn
Franklin Street
Manuka 2603
Telephone (062) 95 1077
PO Box 317
Manuka 2603

The Association of Independent Schools of
   ACT
PO Box 469
Manuka (062) 49 7747 a.h.

Curriculum branch
ACT Schools Authority
O'Connell Education Centre
Stuart Street
Griffith 2603
Telephone (069) 95 4387

Counselling services:
Guidance and Counselling Section Schools
   Branch
ACT Schools Authority
PO Box 20
Civic Square 2608
Telephone (062) 49 0235

Assessment of students:
Guidance and Counselling Section (see above)

Counselling services:
Counselling, Guidance and Clinical Services
   (centres located in each region)
Head Office
334 Queensbury Street

Carlton 3053
Telephone (03) 341 4111
Special Education Unit personnel
Pupil welfare officers

Assessment of students:
Counselling, Guidance and Clinical Services
   (address as above)
Special Education Unit personnel

Gifted Children Task Force
PO Box 523
Camberwell 3124
Telephone (03) 82 7487 and (03) 813 3164

Tertiary education:
Contact the education faculty within each
   tertiary institution

Victoria

Equal opportunity issues/education of girls:
Coordinator for the Elimination of Sexism in
   Schools
Victorian Department of Education
Office of the Director-General of Education
2 Treasury Place
Melbourne 3000
Telephone (03) 651 2587

Victorian Catholic Education Commission
383 Albert Street
East Melbourne 3002
Telephone (03) 654 2199

Association of Independent Schools of Victoria
Mercer House
82 Jolimont Street
Jolimont 3002
Telephone (03) 654 4322

Queensland

Department of Education
Senior Research Officer
Curriculum Branch
Planning and Services Division
Department of Education
PO Box 33
North Quay 4000
Telephone (07) 224 7914

Regional directors of education within each
   region may also be contacted.

Department Committee on Provision for
   Gifted and Talented Children
Contact the Senior Research Officer
Curriculum Branch (address and telephone as
   above).

Counselling services:
Head Office
Guidance Section
Division of Special Education
Department of Education
PO Box 33
Brisbane North Quay 4000
Telephone (07) 44 6851

Regional guidance officers — contact regional
   guidance officers at regional offices of
   education.

Assessment of students:
Guidance Section address as above.
Regional guidance officers at offices of
   Education Department

Queensland Catholic Education Commission
The Catholic Centre
143 Edward Street
Brisbane 4000
Telephone (07) 229 3744
GPO Box 2441
Brisbane 4001

Association of Independent Schools of
   Queensland
Units 16 and 17
67 O'Connell Terrace
Bowen Hills 4006
Telephone (07) 52 2878

Peninsula Enrichment Program for Gifted and
   Talented Children
35 Windemere Road
Albany Creek 4035
Telephone (07) 264 2205

It should be noted that this is but one of a
   number of programs being offered by
   interested groups. Regional offices of
   education have information on those
   currently operating in their regions.

Tertiary education:
Queensland Board of Teacher Education
39 Sherwood Road
Toowong 4066
Telephone (07) 370 7168

South Australia

Education Department of South Australia
Senior Education Officer
Special Education
3rd Floor Education Centre
31 Flinders Street
Adelaide 5000
Telephone (08) 227 1790

Counselling services:
Education Department of South Australia

Guidance and Special Services
14th Floor Education Centre
31 Flinders Street
Adelaide 5000
Telephone (08) 227 2172

Regional guidance officers based within each
   region

School counsellors

Assessment of students:
Guidance and Special Services
Regional guidance officers

Equal opportunity issues/education of girls:
Women's Advisory Unit
Education Department of South Australia
31 Flinders Street
Adelaide 5000
Telephone (08) 227 3876

South Australian Commission for Catholic
   Schools
47 Waymouth Street
Adelaide 5000
Telephone (08) 212 2261
GPO Box 2149
Adelaide 5001

The Association of Independent Schools of
South Australia Inc.
2 Clarke Street
Norwood 5067
Telephone (08) 332 2922

Tertiary education:
Tertiary Education Authority of South
Australia
18 Dequetteville Terrace
Kent Town 5067
Telephone (08) 42 7951

Northern Territory

Gifted children's program
Senior Education Officer
Professional Services Branch
Department of Education
PMB 25
Winnellie 5789
Telephone (089) 85 0211

Northern Territory Catholic Education Office
Diocesan Centre
Smith Street
Darwin 5790
Telephone (089) 81 8258

Equal opportunity issues/education of girls:
Coordinator for the Elimination of Sexism in
Education
Department of Education
Professional Services Branch
Chrisp Street
Rapid Creek 5792
Telephone (089) 85 0211

Counselling services:
Student Services
Department of Education
GPO Box 4821
Darwin 5794
Telephone (089) 80 4211

School counsellors

Assessment of students:
Guidance officers attached to Student Services

Education Unlimited
PO Box 1532
Darwin 5794
and PO Box 1728
Alice Springs 5750

Tertiary education:
Northern Territory Post School Advisory
Council
PO Box 529
Darwin 5794
Telephone (089) 80 4211

Western Australia

Gifted and Talented Children's Program
Project Group
Superintendent
Gifted and Talented Children
Education Department
151 Royal Street
East Perth 6000
Telephone (09) 420 4513

Counselling services:
Gifted and Talented Children's Program
Project Group
Counselling, Guidance and Clinical Services
151 Royal Street
East Perth 6000
Telephone (09) 420 4663

Assessment of students:
Gifted and Talented Children's Program
Project Group
School guidance officers

Equal opportunity issues/education of girls:
Coordinator for Equal Opportunity
Education Department
151 Royal Street
East Perth 6000
Telephone (09) 420 4653

Tertiary education:
Western Australian Post-Secondary Education
    Commission
16–18 Stirling Highway
Nedlands 6009
Telephone (09) 386 6355

Association of Independent Schools of Western
    Australia (Inc.)
Mr W. R. Dickinson
c/o Scotch College
76 Shenton Road
Swanbourne 6010

Mr B. R. Scott
PO Box 254
Subiaco 6008
Telephone (09) 381 5277

Western Australia Catholic Education
    Commission
6 Salvado Road
Wembley 6014
Telephone (09) 381 5444 or (09) 381 6764
PO Box 254
Subiaco 6008

Tasmania

A Working Party Report was produced in 1982
and circulated for comment. The Education
Department examined reactions to this Report
and announced its policy in 1984.

An incorporated body called 'Explorers
Unlimited Inc.' was formed at the time of a visit
to Hobart by Henry Collis, World President of
the Council for Gifted and Talented Children
in 1978. This body promotes and encourages
activities which cater for out-of-school interests
of children.

Counselling services:
The Guidance Services branch provides
    counselling services in all regions.

Assessment of students:
The work of Guidance Services is
    supplemented by the testing section of the
    Curriculum Branch.

Equal opportunity issues/education of girls:
Improving Education for Girls Project
Curriculum Centre
Education Department
57 Brisbane Street
Hobart 7000
Telephone (002) 30 6409

The Association of Independent Schools of
    Tasmania
Room 210
86 Murray Street
Hobart 7000
Telephone (002) 30 3923

Tertiary education:
Tertiary Education Commission of Tasmania
GPO Box 329
Hobart 7001
Telephone (003) 26 0536

Tasmanian Catholic Education Commission
430 Elizabeth Street
North Hobart 7002
Telephone (002) 34 6027
PO Box 102
North Hobart 7002

SPECIAL PROVISION FOR THE TALENTED IN VARIOUS STATES

Attempts are being made to cater for the needs of gifted and talented children in our schools. I have enclosed the following summary of activities. My thanks go to the South Australian Department of Education for assistance in compiling this list from their excellent booklet, *Children with Gifts and Talents: Questions and Answers.*

A complete discussion of provisions for the talented in state schools may be obtained from Dr Eddie Braggett's book, *Education of Gifted and Talented Children: Australian Provision*, published by the Schools' Commission and available at Government bookshops.

New South Wales

General school provisions:
Specialist music high school and performing arts high school
Opportunity classes for selected academically gifted within certain primary schools
Selective high schools
Country Assistance Program camps
Saturday classes and after school classes organised at regional levels.
Internal school provision

Support groups and resources:
State Coordinating Committee for the Education of the Talented Child

Regional consultants Policy document and related support documents: *Needs, characteristics and support; Identification; School policy and organisation; Curriculum and teaching; Parents and the community.*

Curriculum materials such as Special interest units available from ABC

New South Wales Association for Gifted and Talented Children
Personnel within tertiary institutions
Enrichment weekends organised by the Mitchell Advanced Education
Enrichment camps organised by the Riverina Murray Institute of Higher Education

Australian Capital Territory

General school provisions:
A number of schools have special programs in this area.

Support groups:
Inservice programs have been organised by the Professional Development Section to increase awareness and understanding of teachers.

Victoria

General school provision:
Post primary
Five select entry specialist music schools
One select entry music dance school
Three select entry high academic performance schools
Acceleration project of University High School
Cluster groups of schools
Mentor contact register
Project R.A.F.T.
Primary
Individual student programs, withdrawal programs etc.

Camps:
Camps for such subject areas as music and mathematics are organised at regional and state levels.

Support groups:
Gifted Children Task Force
Special assistance resource teachers
Cluster group support
Special Education Units located in each sub-region
District contact: people in primary schools
Gifted Children Committee
Victorian Association for Gifted and Talented Children
Personnel within tertiary institutions

Queensland

General school provisions:
Part-time withdrawal classes
Electives
In-class enrichment

Camps:
Camps such as a writers' camp and a camp for musically outstanding students organised at regional and state levels.

Support groups:
Subject advisory teachers
Regional library advisers
Queensland Association for Gifted and Talented Children
Peninsula Enrichment Program for Gifted and Talented Children
Personnel within tertiary institutions

South Australia

General school provisions:
Junior primary/primary —
Part-time withdrawal classes
In-class enrichment
Acceleration
Mentor system
Electives
Secondary —
Individual timetabling
Electives
Cluster groups of schools

Mentors
Artists in residence
Four special interest centres (music)
One special interest centre (languages)

Support groups:
Senior Education Officer (Special Education)
Regional support teachers based at Special Education Units
Special Education Unit personnel
Adaptive education teachers
Subject advisers and consultants
South Australian Association for Gifted and Talented Children
Personnel within tertiary institutions

Northern Territory

Gifted Children's Policy (1983)

School based initiatives:
Full-time units
Part-time withdrawal classes
In-class enrichment
Dripstone High School differentiated program

Western Australia

General school provisions:
Primary —
School based programs (years 1–3)
Special interest centres (years 4–5)
Full-time extension classes (years 6–7)
Secondary —
Secondary special placement programs (years 8–12)
The target group for each of the above provisions is identified through teacher, parent and student nomination procedures, the use of standardised tests and information relevant to the performance of each child.

Camps:
Weekend special focus camps and vocation camps are organised by the Project Group and provide students with a wide range of intellectually challenging experiences.

Support groups:
Gifted and Talented Children's Program
Project Group
Regional coordinators
Advisory teachers
Gifted and Talented Children's Association of
  Western Australia
Personnel within tertiary institutions.

Tasmania

General school provisions:
Schools have been influenced by initiatives
  taken interstate and overseas. School based
curriculum developments include programs
for gifted and talented students.
A music scholarship scheme to provide four
years of special tuition in music has been
available for some years.

Support of teachers:
There is system support for curriculum development to provide for individual interests
and needs of students. This support is being
used by some schools to cater for particular
needs of the talented and gifted.
A consultant has been appointed in one pilot
program to support initiatives in a cluster of
primary schools.

BOOK LIST

This a comprehensive list of books about bringing up bright children. I have marked with an asterisk those I found particularly useful.

A good variety of activity books is available from book shops and newsagents. These books are generally quite cheap and usually cover mathematical puzzles and games, language, science and general knowledge. Keep your eyes open for such books, especially at fetes and 'el cheapo' shops.

Abidin, Richard *Parenting Skills* (Human Sciences Press, 1976)

Abraham, W. *Gifts, Talents and the Very Young* (Ventura County Press, 1977)

Beck, Joan *How to Raise a Brighter Child* (Penguin, 1974)

Becker, Wesley *Parents are Teachers* (Research Press, 1971)

Belliston, L. and M. *How to Raise a More Creative Child* (Argus Communications, 1982)

Berger, Gilda How to Raise a Brighter Child (Collins, 1980)

*Braggett, Eddie *Curriculum for Gifted and Talented Children* (Schools Commission, 1983)

Braggett, Eddie *Education of Gifted and Talented Children — An Australian Provision* (Schools Commission, 1986)

Briggs, D. *Your Child's Self Esteem* (Doubleday Dolphin, 1975)

Burns, Marilyn *The Book of Think* (Brawa Book Company, 1976)

*Clark, Barbara *Growing up Gifted* (Merrill, 1983)

Coffey, K. *Parentspeak* (Ventura County Press, 1976)

*Congdon, Peter *Children of High Ability, Finding and Helping Them* (Solihull, 1979)
Available from Ballarat Community Education Centre, PO Box 223E Ballarat East, 3350)

Dalton, Joan *Adventures in Thinking* (Nelson, 1986)

Davitz, L. *How to Live Almost Happy with a Teenager* (Winston, 1983)

*De Bono, E. *Children Solve Problems* (Pelican, 1982)

Delp, J. and Martinson, R. A. *Handbook for the Parents of the Gifted and Talented* (Ventura County Press, 1977)

Dirkmeyer, D. and McKay, G. *Systematic Training for Effective Parenting* (American Guidance Service, 1982)

Dobson, J. *Preparing for Adolescence* (Bantam, 1978)

Eales, Connie *Raising Your Talented Child* (Fontana, 1983)

Fellcer, R. *A Parents' Guide to the Education of Pre-school Gifted Children* (National Assocation of State Boards of Education, 1978)

*Gallagher, J. J. *Teaching Gifted Children* (Allyn and Bacon, 1975)

Ginsberg, G. and Harrison, C. *How to Help Your Gifted Child* (Monarch, 1977)

Growan, J. 'Twenty-five suggestions for parents of able children' in *Gifted Child Quarterly,* volume 8 pp 192–193 (National Association for Gifted Children, 1962)

Hopkinson, D. *The Education of Gifted Children* (Woburn Press, 1978)

Kauigher, H. *Everyday Enrichment for Gifted Children at Home and School* (Ventura County Press, 1977)

Kaplan, S. *Education of the Pre-school/Primary Gifted and Talented* (Ventura County Press, 1977)

Karnes, M. *The Understanding of Our Young Gifted Children* (Council for Exceptional Children, 1983)

Laycock, F. *Gifted Children* (Scott Foresman, 1979)

Lewis, D. *How to be a Gifted Parent* (Jan. 1979)

*Noller, R.; Parnes, S. and Biendi, A. *Creative Action Book* (Charles Schriebner Sons, 1976)

*Painter, F. *Living with a Gifted Child* (Souvenir Press, 1984)

Pickard, Phyllis *If You Think Your Child is Gifted* (Allen and Unwin, 1976)

Training Manual for Volunteer Counsellors (Queensland Association for Gifted and Talented Children, 1985)

Raph, Jane et al *Bright Underachievers* (Teachers' College Press of Columbia University, 1969)

*Roeder, W. *Gifted Young Children* (Teachers' College Press, 1985)

*Shasta County *Gateway — Towards Understanding the Gifted and Talented* (A Handbook for Parents) (Shasta County Press)

Silverman, M. and Wheelan, S. *How to Discipline Without Feeling Guilty* (Research Press, 1980)

' Taylor, B. *Dear Mom and Dad. Parents and the Pre-school* (Birmingham University Press, 1978)

*Tempest, N. R. *Teaching Clever Children* (Routledge Kegan Paul, 1974)

Webb, J. *Guiding the Gifted Child* (Australian Association for Gifted and Talented Children, 1980)

Up-to-date Periodicals

Chalkface — available from Subscriptions Co-ordinator Government Printing Officer, PO Box 203, North Melbourne Victoria 3041. Subscription $4.55 pa.

Gateway — available from Academic Extension Branch of Western Australian Department of Education, 151 Royal Street, East Perth WA 6000.

TalentEd — available from Armidale CAE, Armidale NSW 2350. Subscription $6 pa.

KITS

Catering for the Talented — published by the Sidney Meyer Foundation. All state primary schools in New South Wales and Victoria were issued with this kit. Ask your school principal if you may borrow a copy.

Children with Gifts and Talents: Questions and Answers (An Information Booklet for Parents) — published by the South Australian Department of Education and available from government bookshops and some Education Centres.

Creative Activities for Very Able Readers — obtainable from the Learning Enrichment Centre, Special Education and Guidance Services, 117 Agnew Street, Norman Park Queensland 4170. For primary level students.

Pick and Choose Package for Active Eager Youngsters — published by the New South Wales Department of Education. This kit contains idea cards, activity cards and cassettes.

Talented Children and Teaching Strategies for Talented Students — available from the Continuing Education Cassette Service, University of New South Wales, PO Box 1, Kensington NSW 2033. For primary level students.

Units of Work for Talented Children — available from the New South Wales Department of Education Teaching Resources, 2 Railway Parade, Burwood NSW 2134.

Various resource materials available on request — diverse areas of problem solving such as collecting and organising data, analysis, computer literacy; obtainable from Creative Thinking Resources, PO Box 22, Northbridge NSW 2063.